"In this age of discord and disconnection, s[...] with others on even the most basic level [...] Jeanne Martinet wisely advises readers on h[...] est social landmines with skill, grace, and humor. The strategies and advice in this book are timely, relevant, and actionable; this is the *adulting* manual I want to give to everyone I know!"

— **Carla Naumburg, PhD**, author of *How to Stop Losing Your Sh*t with Your Kids*

"In *Mingling with the Enemy*, Jeanne Martinet offers a powerful antidote to rising incivility, intolerance, and outright hate. This insightful book is lucid, compelling, and above all, timely."

— **Maggie Jackson**, author of *Distracted*

"*Mingling with the Enemy* is a timely and useful book. Martinet does a wonderful job of exposing the social costs of our polarized era, and she offers a number of sensible tips for helping us, if not overcome our differences, at least learn to understand them better. Civil conversation of course is not a cure-all, but, as Martinet shows, it is a necessary step toward a more productive political discourse—and a step away from the brink."

— **Ulrich Boser**, author of *The Leap*

"Jeanne Martinet offers a much-needed guide to surviving today's growing 'partisan phobia.' Using examples from everyday social situations, Martinet outlines clever and practical tools to help navigate, and even disarm, politically divisive topics. Her fun, conversational style makes this an enjoyable and accessible read for anyone who is tired of fighting, and instead wants to connect more meaningfully across the aisle."

— **Anatasia S. Kim, PhD**, associate professor of clinical psychology at The Wright Institute in Berkeley, CA; and author of *It's Time to Talk (and Listen)*

MINGLING

with the

ENEMY

A Social

Survival Guide

for Our

Divided Era

JEANNE MARTINET

New Harbinger Publications, Inc.

O'Neal Library
50 Oak Street
Mountain Brook, AL 35213

1772

Publisher's Note

This publication is designed to provide accurate and authoritative information in regard to the subject matter covered. It is sold with the understanding that the publisher is not engaged in rendering psychological, financial, legal, or other professional services. If expert assistance or counseling is needed, the services of a competent professional should be sought.

Distributed in Canada by Raincoast Books

Copyright © 2020 by Jeanne Martinet
New Harbinger Publications, Inc.
5674 Shattuck Avenue
Oakland, CA 94609
www.newharbinger.com

Cover design by Amy Shoup

Acquired by Jennye Garibaldi

Edited by Rona Bernstein

All Rights Reserved

Library of Congress Cataloging-in-Publication Data

Names: Martinet. Jeanne - author.
Title: Mingling with the enemy : a social survival guide for our politically divided era / Jeanne Martinet.
Description: Oakland, CA : New Harbinger Publications, [2020] | Includes bibliographical references.
Identifiers: LCCN 2019055177 (print) | LCCN 2019055178 (ebook) | ISBN 9781684035212 (paperback) | ISBN 9781684035229 (pdf) | ISBN 9781684035236 (epub)
Subjects: LCSH: Conversation. | Conversation--Political aspects. | Interpersonal communication. | Interpersonal conflict.
Classification: LCC BJ2121 .M373 2020 (print) | LCC BJ2121 (ebook) | DDC 177/.2--dc23
LC record available at https://lccn.loc.gov/2019055177
LC ebook record available at https://lccn.loc.gov/2019055178

Printed in the United States of America

22   21   20

10   9   8   7   6   5   4   3   2   1   First Printing

O'Neal Library
50 Oak Street
Mountain Brook, AL 35213

Contents

Fear and Loathing at the Dinner Table

I was hosting a dinner party in January of 2018 and had just finished serving the stew and opening the wine when one of my guests asked me what I was working on. I told him my book title: *Mingling with the Enemy.* He clapped his hands in glee. "That's gonna be a winner!" he said. "That's a book we Democrats really need."

Then I explained I was writing it for both a conservative and liberal audience. He looked confused and then his face fell. "What?! That's a terrible idea. You can't do that," he said.

He may have been right. This has been the hardest book I have ever written. Especially since the 2016 election, many Americans regard each other as the enemy, based on how they voted or how they feel about one or more of the issues. To write a book that basically tells people, "No matter what anyone says to you, no matter how wrong you think they are, you must always behave well in social situations" was a formidable task.

I don't pretend to be a political expert. My field of expertise is social mores, social interaction, and the art of conversation. I wrote this book because the country's growing divisiveness is seeping into our social lives, and into all our conversations. Politics are now omnipresent, affecting our ability to enjoy our leisure time the way we used to. I don't want to either encourage or discourage people from talking politics; what I would like is for people of different parties to be able to talk to each other, period—to commune, to mingle, to conduct business together without everything always about to escalate into a major battle.

This is primarily a survival guide, to teach you how to navigate our relatively new social terrain. It's for when you are having a casual conversation and suddenly feel you are being attacked. It's to give you practical strategies when things suddenly blow up in your face. Or when you really feel as though you *must* confront someone about something they've said, even though you know your son's wedding reception is not the place to do it. It's a blueprint for helping you find ways to talk at social events without throwing a fit, for helping you know what to do when you are suddenly pulled into a fight you'd rather not be in.

We can't afford to jettison courtesy, kindness, and good manners. Neither should we decide never to socialize with anyone who disagrees with us. What good is it if we never share a cocktail or join a video chat with anyone who's ever voted on the other side? If we never break bread with someone who we feel is wrong? Politics are infecting our social lives in a way I don't think they should, and in a way that only divides us further.

I'm a Democrat living in Manhattan, but I have friends and relatives I dearly love who are Republicans. There is an underlying tension between us, a tension that sometimes affects our relationships, a tension that is part of the permanent landscape we all now live in. While this book was written before the outbreak of COVID-19, the pandemic has only amplified this tension. It's very easy, even deeply satisfying sometimes, to adopt a "take no prisoners, they're all insane!" attitude during a conversation. We have all done this at some point or another. Indeed, righteous indignation has become our feel-good drug of choice. While I believe that attitude can be valid in the political arena—when people are out there fighting for public policy—when we sit down to socialize, the weapons (though not necessarily your opinions) should be left at the door. And when the other person has not left theirs at the door, at least you need to be armed with the proper defenses.

I spent months trying to figure out how to write this book, and wondering whether I even should. My fear was that I would offend people by writing it wrong. That I would be too partisan in my point of view. That maybe there really is no good solution to that heart-stopping moment when you are standing at a party talking to someone you don't know, and that person suddenly says to you, "Don't tell me you're one of those stupid people who voted for _____?"

I want to emphasize that this advice, these techniques and strategies and lines, are not for use when the purpose of the get-together is to try to rectify local problems on your street or in your town or city, or for any time when serious debate is important or necessary for our democracy or for the betterment of our communities. This book is about your social life. The term "mingling" refers mostly to those times when you are meeting or mixing with a lot of people, often ones you don't know. I'm also not suggesting that we never discuss politics at parties; this is a guide to instruct us how to *not fight* about politics at parties. We need to re-master the art of mingling for today's social climate. Most important, when it comes to facing the "enemy," we need to remember the old adage from Franklin Roosevelt—that the only thing we have to fear is fear itself.

Wait…Franklin Roosevelt? Wasn't he that socialist Democrat who created the pro-regulation, anti-economic growth policies that have completely ruined our country? Or was he the last president we had who was truly looking out for working people and believed that everyone should have a support net for when times get tough? It is my hope that Mingling with the Enemy will help people who hold such opposing points of view raise a glass together and have an engaging conversation—even if one of them is drinking Budweiser and the other is drinking organic kombucha.

Socializing in the Powder Keg Era

It can happen before you even realize you're in danger.

You're at a work-related cocktail party. For once, everything is going swimmingly. You've had fun conversations with several people, a couple of whom might actually benefit your career. You've even met someone you didn't know from your own office who could end up being a friend; you made a lunch date with him for next week. You've had two glasses of wine, you're feeling great, and your shoes don't even hurt. You're standing with three other guests—one a potential client—who have just laughed loudly at one of your favorite restaurant jokes. *Who says large parties are so daunting?* you think happily to yourself. And that's when it happens.

"Speaking of Italian food," says the woman standing across from you. "Was that a statue of Columbus I saw in the park I passed on my way here?"

"Not sure," you say, still inwardly basking in the success of your joke.

Another woman in the group speaks up. "Oh yes, it is Columbus," she says. "By a nineteenth-century Italian sculptor. There's been a lot of recent controversy about it in the liberal media, which I think is utterly ridiculous."

Everyone freezes. It's as though someone has just pulled out a gun. People dart furtive looks at each other. *Uh-oh.*

"Why? Why do you think that's so ridiculous?" says the woman across from you, bristling. "Columbus enslaved every native he ever came across. He certainly shouldn't be celebrated."

Then the man next to you, the potential client, jumps in. "Never mind Columbus. At least that was the fifteenth century. What about the statues commemorating slave owners that are still standing all over the South?" he snaps. And…you're off.

Welcome to mingling in the Powder Keg Era, where everything's always about to blow sky high. No subject is safe now: Weather leads to climate change, sports leads to NFLers' knee protests, asking someone how they are feeling can easily propel the conversation into a dispute on health care. Talking about what your daughter is wearing to prom can become an uncomfortable debate about the #MeToo movement. A perfectly innocent chat about chocolate cake might take a bad turn, and before you know it you find yourself fighting about genetically altered foods. Even talking about someone's children or grandchildren isn't completely innocuous; in a matter of minutes you can be embroiled in an unforeseen argument about the controversial anti-vaccine movement or the public education system.

We have all gotten very issue-y, and always seem to be a trigger word or two away from losing our tempers. Of course, many would say this is as it should be—that it's about time people started caring more about the problems of the world, especially now that there's so much at stake. But while the image of powerful world leaders with their fingers on the proverbial "button" is a terrifying one, the truth is we all have our own fingers on the button these days. A couple of decades ago we weren't walking on eggshells all the time. Now, the slightest wrong step and we are all yelling at each other—or withdrawing into awkward silences. It's not that there haven't always been combustible topics. It just seems as though now almost everything has become a combustible topic.

It's no secret that our country is more politically divided than it has been since the Civil War. According to a 2016 Pew Research study, 81 percent of Democrats have an unfavorable opinion of the Republican Party; the exact same percentage of Republicans feel that way about the Democratic Party. Moreover, 55 percent of Democrats say the Republican Party makes them "afraid," while 49 percent of Republicans say the same about the Democratic Party.[1] Naturally, this schism turns a lot of social functions into potential battlegrounds. And yes, there have always been political disagreements at social functions; otherwise, the old adage about never talking politics or religion at the dinner table would not exist. But now we are experiencing a relatively new, increasingly intense ideological polarization, and it's become virtually impossible to avoid talking politics. While there are a lot of theories about why this is happening, I think it is at least partly because we are all being pummeled by news twenty-four hours a day, because we are not all sourcing the same news, and because many people are only exposed to information that is tailor-made to support their existing belief system.

I myself lean to the left, so I tend to believe that media outlets like *The New York Times* and *The Washington Post* are more or less objective and factual, and that many people on the right are getting distorted news (or no news). However, I am well aware that there are a lot of conservatives who are every bit as convinced that *I* am the one who is getting biased or "fake" news. Perhaps more to the point, I know many people on both sides who will be furious with me for daring to make a comparison that implies anything like equal responsibility for this rift. Both conservatives and liberals (the true zealots, at least) don't just think but know for certain that *they* are the ones who are armed with the facts, and the other side is deluded—victims of pernicious propaganda, or simply out of touch with reality. Add to this apparently unsolvable paradigm our sound-bitten, social-media-imbued perspectives, and there are no gray areas left, only black and white. You're in, or you're out. You're *for* whatever the current hashtag movement or sentiment is, or you're *against* it. Diatribe has replaced dialogue. It's the Hatfields and the McCoys—on a grand scale.

This sense of urgency and fear is fueling social clashes not only between conservatives and liberals. I don't think there has ever been a time when people within the same camp have disagreed so much. During the 2016 primaries, I witnessed arguments at dinner tables about Bernie versus Hillary that were every bit as vehement as the fiercest two-party fights. (By all accounts, there were similar arguments at conservatives' get-togethers about Trump—versus anyone else.) These days, you just never know when a conversation is going to take an uncomfortable turn. It's very easy to make an incorrect assumption about where another person stands on a certain issue. Two neighbors who may have voted for the same congressional candidate can still find themselves arguing about local zoning laws, traffic regulations, school policies, or composting. Topics like abortion, religion, and animal rights often cross party lines. Also, there are a lot of terms that older people use without even thinking—terms that are deeply offensive to the younger generation.

For that matter, conversational trouble spots are not limited to politics. Partly because of how social media has changed the way society absorbs and reacts to data, we have become super-definite about everything, no matter how trivial. What used to be fodder for playful conversational debate is now often impetus for defending our own personal convictions. People are having serious arguments about the proper way to cook a turkey, whether *Star Wars* is less or more moral than *Star Trek*, whether bicycle riders should have to have licenses, or whether a martini is made with gin or vodka. (It's with gin, people!) I once heard two people arguing about Samsung phones versus Apple; one vowed to "never date anyone who did not have an iPhone." We are all in our own little worldview bubbles, and we can obtain constant confirmation that ours is the right way from our handheld devices, preprogrammed by us to provide that confirmation. The internet often serves to stroke our egos and inflame our passions rather than inform our minds. Unfortunately, it has also affected our manners.

Civility is disappearing from our social interactions. The ever-escalating rhetoric on Facebook and Twitter—indeed, the general tenor of comments on most social media sites—not only reflects the intensely widening schism in our ideologies, but also illustrates the erosion of courtesy and compassion. Continually stirred up, we are losing the ability, even the desire, to actually talk to each other. In fact, one of the most regrettable casualties of life in the Powder Keg Era is our social lives. The time-honored art of conversation is in danger of extinction, and we are now frequently mangling our mingling.

From years of writing in this field I know that the majority of Americans already suffer from "minglephobia"—the secret terror of talking to strangers at parties; many people are so shy that all strangers seem like potential "enemies." But now there's a whole new level of anxiety about socializing. Now, in addition to minglephobia, we have partisan phobia. This charged, defensive atmosphere is causing people to be even more apprehensive about attending certain affairs; and when they do attend, they are ultra-nervous about saying the wrong thing. Many of us are all too aware that there is now a very short conversational distance between "How are you, what have you been up to, Sally?" and "What?! Seriously??? How can you actually believe that!????" But it's important that we not forgo face-to-face interactions, especially just to avoid potential conflict. (For one thing, we will all end up hermits with bad hair and screen-burned eyes.)

Learning to mingle with the "enemy" is about figuring out how to have conversations with people that may make us afraid or angry. It's about recognizing the presumptions—even prejudices—we may have about other people. It's about letting go of our resistance, being willing to enter into conversations to see where they go. It's about learning to listen more. I suspect we used to be able to handle ourselves better in moments of contention. More of us knew how to see conversational debate as a kind of sparring that was exhilarating—interesting and stimulating more than upsetting and depressing—and let inflammatory comments pass by more easily. I'm pretty sure thirty years ago you could have a spirited discussion about whether or not Columbus should be memorialized with statues without it ending up in bitter remarks or tension-filled silence. Now it's as if we are all battle-scarred soldiers, ever alert for that next attack. And of course, the more unknown the territory, the greater the fear.

Certainly, Thanksgiving dinner has become a stomach-knotting nightmare for many. But when it comes to family dinners, most people know more or less what they are in for. On the other hand, there are countless occasions and settings where you don't necessarily know what the other guests' beliefs or political persuasions are—for example, office parties, business conventions and trade show events, bars and restaurants, weddings, block parties, reunions, PTA events, even doctor's offices. (Remember: just because you are in San Francisco doesn't guarantee the person next to you on the bus did not vote for Trump, and just because you are in Lubbock, Texas doesn't mean there's not a liberal working in the next cubicle.) These unknown arenas can be the scariest, because you are often caught off guard.

In the best of circumstances about 90 percent of us are afraid to walk into a room full of strangers. But now people seem reluctant to go out at all unless it's to be with people in their own circle. This tribalism is affecting our social health and is ultimately bad for society; we're going backward, retreating inward instead of reaching outward. The best kind of socializing should lead to meeting new people, forming new relationships, expanding minds, hearing different ideas, getting new information, having more laughter! When the world is in crisis there is an even greater need for playful conversation and connection. In other words, we need to keep practicing the art of mingling.

How do we go about doing this? By being prepared and training ourselves, by becoming both more skilled at socializing and less defensive. We have to start becoming more interested in what makes each other tick. We need to open up and leave our comforting, familiar fulminations at the door. Conversation that is the most rewarding and fun is conversation that is allowed to roam free—allowed to go where it wants to go, without preconceptions. So we must find a way to let out our creativity—to speak our hearts in some sense, but still engage in a nonconfrontational way with the people in front of us.

Believe it or not, there are easy-to-learn strategies and techniques that can help you navigate even the most difficult conversational hurdles. From my own experience, by interviewing hundreds of people and by consulting well-known experts in the fields of sociology, psychology, etiquette, and humor, I have put together this guide to mingling with whomever we think of as "the enemy." There are a myriad of effective maneuvers—even simple lines—for getting derailed conversations back on track. You can also develop skills that will keep any one negative interaction from ruining your good time. (I am certainly not encouraging anyone to carry on a lengthy conversation with someone whose views they find completely abhorrent.) This book will teach you effective methods for how to keep your mind open, know your own triggers, pick the best topics, test for fanaticism, be an active listener, master the ability to yield without losing, employ humor and storytelling to ease tension, go undercover when necessary, be a brilliant subject changer, find common ground, and escape gracefully. Armed with the right tools, you need not be afraid of any conversational pothole or pitfall. You will be able to handle anything that comes your way.

I can just hear some of you thinking, *Techniques? Skills? This is all wrong. If everyone just said what they really thought all the time, was completely honest, we'd all be a lot better off. Repressing, hiding our true convictions, is the problem with our culture.* Well, all you have to do is read about famous diplomats throughout history to realize it's far more complex than that. Connections have to be made and relationships have to be built on mutual respect and common interests before any inroads are ever made. And here's the thing: Maybe you're right. Maybe this fellow party guest's beliefs are contributing to what you feel is the downfall of humanity. Okay, now what? Will telling him exactly what you think of him while you are both at your friend's graduation soiree really make it better?

After all, even when you are mingling with people of like minds, people whose values are identical to yours, there is still some finesse—even artifice—involved in "working the room." You never navigate a party full of people by telling the complete truth every minute. The fabric of society is held together by an intricate weaving of gentle deceptions and subterfuges. For example, you don't just say to a boring person, "I really don't want to talk to you." You say, "My hostess is signaling me," or "It's been nice to talk to you but I need to use the restroom." And while it's true that social ability seems to come more easily to some than others, most people have to practice in order to develop a knack.

Please rest assured: using my system for mingling with the enemy at a social event doesn't mean you still shouldn't stick to, write about, and work for what you believe in your day-to-day life with all your heart. Using artfulness when you find yourself in challenging social situations does not require that you give up your ideals or compromise on what you believe. But mingling at large affairs can be a little like traveling in foreign lands. When traveling, you have to be ready for the unexpected, aware that sometimes the locals have ideas and opinions you may not be used to, or even find repellent. You have to adopt a bit of an anthropologist's perspective when socializing, and also remember that we have more in common with each other than we often realize—or that at least we almost always have *something* in common, even if it's just a shared love of banjo music. When you can really engage with the other side in the right way, with mutual respect, occasionally someone's mind does change, or open up just a crack. (And don't be shocked if, just once in a while, it turns out to be yours!)

Of course, there are many people who would never think of fighting about issues of any kind at a party, who would never lose their self-control about politics. They either find it easy to stay away from "dangerous" subjects or love to engage respectfully in spirited political sparring. But no matter who you are, in these volatile times you never know when you are going to—unexpectedly—be faced with something you are not prepared or predisposed to deal with. If you can master the art of mingling with the enemy, you will be much less likely to give in to panic. You will not have to turn tail and run, and risk missing out on meeting someone who could enhance your life—or at the very least miss a conversation that would enhance your evening.

There's a fundamental principle to remember as you begin to learn how to mingle with the enemy: Your primary purpose in any mingling situation is to connect with people, not to be right. Whether you are at a business affair or a neighbor's party, whether you are socializing for love, friendship, or career advancement (unless, of course, you are at a political event), your first goal must be interacting with and learning about other human beings. We all have a deep desire for human connection. Conversation is one of life's greatest pleasures. The more people you meet and connect with, the more potential you have for happiness. In other words, the more you mingle, the better your life will be. Venturing forth to mingle with those who may seem like your enemy is really about facing fear—that's the way you can really win.

The first step when you enter a room is to tell yourself that very few people you will ever meet are truly "the enemy." Most people are complicated, multifaceted; one aspect of their personality might make you angry, while another aspect might fascinate you. Within the social realm, we need to put exploring before battling. There's an old saying: People you haven't met yet are just the friends you don't know. I know that sounds impossibly Pollyannaish. But the fact that we can't get along is really just a reflection of the human condition; we are all isolated in our own bodies, thinking that no one will understand us, or that we will never understand them—that it's not even worth trying. But it *is* worth trying. So be brave and go forth. And if you do come across the enemy while on the mingling battlefield, I hope this book will provide you with all the equipment you need for succeeding beyond your expectations.

Ready? Here we go—into the fray!

By failing to prepare,
you are preparing to fail.

—Benjamin Franklin

CHAPTER ONE

Pre-Mingle Prep

So how can you prepare yourself for your possibly problematic face-to-face interactions? How do you let go of your fears and get yourself in the right frame of mind for these social adventures?

First, you have to welcome the idea of *going* to the gathering. Let's say you've been invited to your in-laws' annual July 4th barbecue, and you are pretty sure many of the other guests are ardent supporters of someone you vehemently despise. Or perhaps you are expected to attend an orientation mixer at a business conference in a state that is 80 percent the opposite political persuasion from yours. Why even bother showing up, you may ask? Why put yourself through it? You are probably just going to lose your cool if you go, so it's better to just stay in, right?

Wrong. Whenever possible, *always go to the party.* You never know who is going to be there, no matter what your expectations are. There could be at least one other person there with whom you could have a fabulous conversation, or develop a useful business connection. Also, your preconceptions about the group you are about to encounter are probably not entirely accurate. We have let our divided perspectives blind us to the fact that most people are not all one thing or another. If the event is for work, you may more or less be forced to mingle with the enemy, but even if it is not a business function, know that you can always be in control of when and if—and how—you decide to talk about politics or any other touchy subject.

Whether you are expecting to interact with the enemy or not, it's always best to try to enter into every social scenario with an open mind and heart—eager to investigate, experience, and engage. However, situations where you suspect you will be potentially mingling with people who have strong opposite life views or political bents can be especially anxiety producing, and it is going to go a lot better if you are psychologically prepared. One way you can do this is to practice a bit of the art of mindfulness—to try to get centered beforehand. Another is to get rid of mindsets that may not be helpful and to be aware of any hot button issues you may have.

The first step? Understanding the influence of social media.

THE DANGERS OF "ANTI-SOCIAL" MEDIA

One thing that will most assuredly not help you get ready for mingling with the enemy is spending a lot of time on social media. I confess that when I first heard the term "social media" back in 2005 or 6, I was genuinely perplexed. It seemed an oxymoronic term. To me the word "social" connotes physically being with other people—as in real-life activities where people meet each other—not sitting alone at a computer. Believe me, I am no Luddite. I am as addicted to my smartphone as the next person. But the truth is that the internet has decreased our face-to-face time.

The average American spends twenty-four hours a week online, according to a recent study by USC Annenberg.[2] There are many other studies that suggest that social media in particular is deleterious to our social and emotional health, and that it contributes to the dramatic political rift that is taking place. One such study, published in the *Harvard Business Review* in 2017, revealed that increased use of Facebook was negatively associated with overall well-being, especially mental health.[3] Another recent study by researchers at Stanford and New York University revealed that people who use Facebook regularly are more politically polarized on the issues than those who are not using Facebook at all[4] (and the researchers had to pay people to stay off Facebook).

It's easy enough to see how sites like Facebook and Twitter have become a factor in the polarization of society, as they are apt to heighten our more negative emotions—fear and anger. We've always had political arguments, but most social media sites tend to tap into and encourage our basest instincts. Trying to have a meaningful conversation on social media—especially if it is with someone you disagree with—is like trying to build a sandcastle in a hurricane.

This is not to say that social media does not have value. It's great for organizing events, getting instantaneous news on global events, and a million other things. But the real danger is that it gives us the illusion that we are more connected with each other. We are supplied with numbers that indicate we have a large circle of contacts, larger than we could ever achieve without the internet, but exactly what kind of connecting are we doing?

To my mind there are five basic aspects of social media that make it detrimental to our social health. First, there's the feeling of *anonymity*, of facelessness. In the digital world it can be hard to remember that the posts you see are attached to real humans. It's easy to dehumanize the other person. This "remote" aspect of social media allows people's ids to roam wild. The screaming matches people get into in the comments section of an article or a post often sink to a level that would never happen in real life. This is partly because so much of real-life, face-to-face communication is nonverbal and partly because we don't directly experience the effect of our words on the other person.

Second, there is the *immediacy* of the internet. The medium encourages people to respond right away, so that they often end up conveying a purely emotional reaction. Many people do not take the time to think about or edit what they say. Millennials and Gen Zs may not remember what drunk dialing was like, but this is a million times worse. With drunk dialing you only humiliated yourself in front of one person, and there was no permanent record of it for all to see.

Then there is the sheer *volume* of content. The amount of sound bites—opinions, quips, insults, jokes, excerpts, links—that we are confronted with numbs our social sensibilities. It's both overwhelming and distracting. How many of us would have time for other activities if we were not constantly on Facebook and Twitter and Instagram? If you are a political person but are spending multiple hours arguing with people online, it's probably not helping anybody; it's not serving you and not even serving whatever cause it is you are posting about.

The fourth problem is that most information is *not vetted* in any way; social media promotes what some have called (if they're putting a positive spin on it) "citizen journalism." Everyone is weighing in. Everyone is a warrior for the truth. Everyone is a commentator and everyone is an expert. We now all live with the notion that everyone's opinion is equal to everyone else's. So Joe's blog carries the same weight as *The Wall Street Journal*. Social media posts are organized for the most part by popularity instead of veracity or level of importance. People have quickly learned that hyperpartisan and inflammatory comments command more attention than more nuanced or subtle comments, and many use teaser links called "clickbait" to lure people to even more provocative content. This is the arena where disinformation can flourish and false beliefs can be fed. Social media is fertile ground for various hate groups to operate successfully.

Last and perhaps most important, there is the *narcissistic bubble* aspect of social media. Thanks in part to the brilliance of search engine algorithms like Google, our devices know what we like and will happily feed it to us. So (1) we naturally seek out what is already in our own belief system, and (2) the internet actively guides us to more of the same. On Twitter or Facebook, we curate our own news. A few decades ago you would turn on one of the three TV network news stations, and you'd get (basically) the global headlines, the national news, and any other science or local item of interest. You did not choose what news to consume; there were experts whose job it was to sift through everything and present it. In this way you would "accidently" get exposed to news about things you might not have known you were interested in. In contrast, social media and the internet basically reflect back our own point of view, rather than offering new information. It is instinctive for us to seek out people who believe what we believe, or who believe what we believe but are more radical in their approach. This reiteration increases our confidence in something we already sort of believe, but it can also intensify that belief. This phenomenon is what social psychologists call the "law of group polarization," which states that if like-minded people are concerned about an issue, their views will become more extreme after discussing it together. Basically is it like an echo chamber, where your words repeat and get louder. It is probably this aspect of social media that has contributed most to the current culture of outrage that makes conversation—online and off—so difficult.

My own personal theory is that cybertechnology came along too soon for our society; human psychological and emotional development were not advanced enough for us to know how to use this power entirely for good. Like a toddler who has been given the power to fly before being able to walk, we are crashing about all over the place, causing damage. I have long referred to sites like Facebook and Twitter as the "anti-social media," because they are one of the reasons people are losing the ability, or at least the desire, to have face-to-face conversations. In spite of the web's limitless power, it's important to remember that even if you see social networking as a positive, it is not the same thing as real-world socializing, and should never take its place.

If you *are* someone who spends a lot of time on social media, especially if you are involved in heated online discussions about the issues, just be aware that when you walk into that cocktail party at 6:00 p.m., you may be bringing in emotional baggage you don't even know you are carrying from some contentious thread you've just been following on Twitter.

Social media certainly isn't going anywhere. But here's my rule of thumb for online conversation: Post your pets, don't post your pet peeves.

EMBRACING SMALL TALK

Small talk is a little like the antipasto or the appetizer of a conversation. It often is followed by a main entrée, but sometimes you can have an entire wonderful and satisfying meal consisting only of appetizers.

Most of us agree we need to get better at talking to each other about important issues, but there is absolutely nothing wrong with sticking to small talk. The fact is, small talk has been given a bad rep. Sometimes, small talk can be a lot better at connecting you to others than "big talk." And after all, connecting is the name of the game. Perhaps talking politics, perhaps not talking politics, but *connecting*. An increasing amount of research shows that small talk (especially with strangers) is good for us, even though most people, when you ask them, think it's a waste of time.

Keep in mind most of the time the reason you are at the party is to meet people, to commune, to mix, to have fun, to get a glimpse into other people's lives and personalities. And that even when you are mingling with the enemy, it's not actually a battle-field. If you were to go to the event thinking you could change people's minds about an issue, that you could help make that corner of the world a better place, I've got news for you: it ain't gonna happen. People's minds do not change about politics or religion during a fifteen-minute conversation. Can you learn something new about how another person thinks or feels? Perhaps. Can you engage in an invigorating sparring back and forth with someone about an important issue? Ideally. It's true that usually the best interactions are when you open up and share how you honestly think and feel about something. But always try to remember that nobody ever wins when you get into a heated argument at a party.

Small talk done well can be like playing a fun game. Maybe you'll never get past the initial small talk, and maybe the small talk will be so much fun it is just fine on its own. The point is it doesn't have to be tedious. Therefore—and this may seem obvious—prepare yourself for some good old-fashioned small talk before you go anywhere near the big talk. ("How do you know the host?" "What part of the city do you live in?" "Have you tasted the chili?" "What do you do for a living?" "What do you like to do in your free time?") Small talk makes everyone less afraid, and will make you feel comfortable with the other person. Once you have broken the ice with a person using small talk, you will have created a kind of conversational bond between you. Then you can choose whether or not to go into more important things. And if you do get into trouble later in the conversation, you can always slide back into the previous small talk. In that way the initial small talk provides a kind of safety net.

UNSET YOUR MIND

Having the "right" mindset, for the most part, simply means not having your mind *pre-set*, at least any more than possible. A mindset is basically a set of attitudes and beliefs. What I mean by it being "pre-set" is having a too rigid sense of identity and personal bias, together with being too attached to the memory of recent social interactions.

What we believe is part of our identity. So we hold on tight to it, especially when we are nervous, as we are when we are entering a room full of strangers, or people we don't know well. We all have a kind of tribal identity, to one degree or another, and there exists a lot of camaraderie and defensiveness around these tribal beliefs. We are usually not conscious of it, but our underlying attitude is "this is what my people believe, everyone I know and trust and love believes this, and how can all those people be wrong?" Your whole identity, your sense of who you are, can seem at risk if someone challenges one of your beliefs.

We are all biased in some way or another. Everyone. I am, you are. For instance, I have a weird prejudice about parents with those big double strollers that are wide instead of long. They take up all the room in the aisle in a store and I find myself thinking,

Who gave them the right to take so much space? I know I'm being totally ridiculous and unfair, and that my feeling could be partly due to my not having had the experience of trying to raise children in Manhattan, where it's the aisles themselves that are really too small. However, because I know this bias is stupid, I never act on it; I always catch myself first.

Knowing what your biases are will help keep your mind flexible during your social interactions. You don't necessarily have to give up your beliefs. While most of the time being biased is not commendable, bias is not always a harmful thing. You could be someone who because of their bias believes poets deserve to get paid as much as bank tellers, or that dogs are inherently superior to cats. Just be aware that you (along with the rest of the world) have some beliefs or opinions that not everyone is going to agree with. And more important, that not everyone who disagrees with you is insane, or evil. Just, perhaps, in your opinion, misinformed. (I mean, really. Who invented those strollers anyway?)

So how do we unset our minds? You really can't, not all the way. But what we *can* try to do is to de-emphasize past conversations. Try to clean-slate your mind and exist in the present. When I visit my Republican friends in Delaware, I try to forget the last conversation I had with them about Hillary. I try to let the conversation unfold anew.

Sometimes it's going to be challenging to keep from reacting to someone you're speaking with—should they, for example, say something indicating that they may vote about an issue the "wrong" way. In other words, it might be hard to continue the conversation and remain interested, and not get distracted by what you see as that person's obvious wrongheadedness and your desire to change their mind at all costs. If you have made an attempt to unset you mind, just a bit—if you have an awareness of your usual pre-set bias, and try to just loosen its hold on you a little—you might be able to listen better and stay in the conversation. If someone were to say something that is so offensive you just simply can't handle it, you will be able to politely extricate yourself from that person (see chapter six).

SPIRITUAL CLIFFSNOTES: GET CENTERED

There is a reason millions of people meditate in the morning. Quieting your mind for ten or fifteen minutes prepares you for the day. People who regularly meditate, pray, or do yoga or tai chi are more able to stay emotionally centered and avoid overreacting. While I don't expect you to change your entire lifestyle by committing to a daily spiritual practice just because you read this book, it's never a bad idea to try to clear your mind before going to any event that is making you nervous. When you feel centered you are less likely to respond defensively. Listening to other points of view will be easier. You will be more able to let someone's inflammatory words wash over you like water.

A lot of people will say to me, "But how can I listen calmly to someone who, by their position on something, is really doing harm to society?" Staying calm does not mean you are betraying anyone, even if what the person is saying is in your opinion wrong. Your intellect is not turned off; you are just able to listen more coolly before responding. Remember, this book is not about letting people win, being a passive doormat, or "turning the other cheek." The techniques in this book will allow you to engage where and when and how you want. It's always your choice whether to discuss a certain topic. But if you follow my rules, you will not succumb to the temptation of becoming defensive or insulting.

There are many philosophers and spiritual teachers who believe there are really only two emotions, two driving forces in all of us: fear and love. As Elizabeth Kubler Ross put it, "All positive emotions come from love, all negative emotions from fear. From love flows happiness, contentment, peace, and joy. From fear comes anger, hate, anxiety and guilt." When you or another person gets angry, you are actually in a state of fear. If this is a valid theory, then we can all avoid getting angry if we can let go of fear. Easier said than done. But this is why so many people are involved in spiritual practices and mindfulness training.

Part of this kind of practice means endeavoring to stay in the present. So tell yourself that tonight you are not going to get seduced into spouting your own favorite sound bites. Perhaps you remember times in the past with your friends when a pithy line got such a good laugh. And maybe it will work again, if you are in the right crowd. But on the other hand, maybe it will *not* be the right thing to say in the current situation. Part of the problem is that we want to be seen as smart; presenting our preorganized thoughts and opinions about the issues of the day is our crutch. Instead, try to stay in the moment. Be alive to the person in front of you; try to hear their words as though it's the first time you've ever heard anyone speak on this subject. At the very least, take a few deep breaths before ringing the doorbell. And remember: keeping a cool head does not mean giving up your passion about any particular issue. Often, it's the people who are speaking quietly and unemotionally that we will listen to the most.

SELF-CHECKLIST: RECOGNIZE YOUR OWN TRIGGERS

The idea of being able to recognize one's own hot buttons in advance, in time to stop the auto-activation of them, is, in one sense, a paradoxical idea. After all, if we could be rational and calm about these things, they would not be triggers for us. The very reason they are hot buttons is they are wired to our sense of personal identity or our past experiences. When a button gets pushed we go on automatic pilot, with no time to think, to consider. People can have triggers about anything—it doesn't have to involve momentous issues of national importance. It can just be a series of unfortunate events leading to a particular sensitivity. I'll never forget the time I came out on the front porch for cocktails during a summer house party with a group of friends. I glanced at one of my friends sitting on the couch, and realized her blouse wasn't zipped in the back.

"Hey, you're not all zipped up there, you know," I said off-handedly, thinking I was helping.

"OH MY GOD! I KNOW I'M NOT ZIPPED, THE ZIPPER IS BROKEN, OKAY?!" she yelled, startling me. What I didn't know was that I was actually the eighth or ninth person who had pointed it out to her, and by the time I said something she was sick of hearing it and ready to blow.

When you are mingling with the enemy, everyone is already a little on guard, so your triggers can be closer to the surface. But triggers are detrimental to conversational flow.

"Reacting emotionally to what another person says is the number one reason conversations turn into arguments," says Michael P. Nichols in his book *The Lost Art of Listening.* "Reactivity is like a child interrupting an adult conversation—it isn't bad, it's inopportune."

The important thing to remember about triggers is that while they are often totally warranted—in other words, it's perfectly understandable for you to be upset—they short circuit us for a few seconds, and that can be bad for a conversation. What we don't want to do is shoot back without thinking. There are basically two kinds of conversational buttons or triggers: current event triggers and preexisting condition triggers.

Current Event Triggers

If there has been a major news event that day, you will probably enter any social situation where you don't know everyone feeling a little rattled or on edge. Maybe it was a shooting, a political scandal, a natural disaster, or a Supreme Court decision, but in this kind of charged atmosphere, the wrong comment can easily light a match and cause an emotional explosion. People are liable to be riled up when something intense has just happened. If you are aware of your emotional state before entering the party, it will be easier to avoid overreaction. Obviously if people have died, being upset is perfectly normal, and to commiserate with others is probably a good thing. On the other hand, if you find yourself directing uncontrollable anger about it to a fellow guest, that is not ideal (even though it certainly happens to all of us at one time or another).

Preexisting Condition Triggers

Let's say that a woman at the party is chatting about her job, and the conversation turns to a sexual discrimination situation that is brewing at her office. If one of the people listening (let's call her Mary) has herself been the victim of gender inequality at work, she is probably going to react more quickly and more emotionally than another person might. What the facts are about this particular discrimination situation may not even matter. This is understandably a hot button for Mary. Similarly, perhaps another guest, John, has a son who is devastated because he got 1600 on his SATs and could not get into his top three college choices, and John is convinced it was because of diversity quotas. If John is talking with someone who happens to mention the efficacy of affirmative action, that might be a trigger for John.

Think back to when you really lost control and regretted it. How did it happen? Have you lost your temper around this subject before? If you know what your own personal triggers are, you can be a little better prepared and perhaps not let yourself be pushed. No matter how justified your feelings about a particular issue are, you want to be in control of your reactions as much as possible, and thereby have the potential for a better, more controlled conversation, one that is not so immediately charged or reactive.

The Trump trigger effect is a unique one. Never have we had a president who pushes quite so many people's buttons. Whether you love him or hate him, Trump is basically a trigger for everyone.

BAD BLOOD WARNING: STAY CLEAR OF OPEN WOUNDS

Remember that even though history repeats itself, you don't necessarily want to. If you've had previous fights with someone who is going to be at this party, try to stay clear of them this time. If your last interaction ended in a screaming match, try not to go there again. Either avoid the person entirely or, when you do interact, talk only about the food on the table and how well the host is looking tonight. Be aware that there is a kind of conversational groove that develops when you disagree with someone about a particular topic more than once. If you talk to the same person about the same thing once again, you will tend to fall into that groove. Later you might even think, "Wait, I should have said such-and-such. That would have really hit my point home. Why did I just repeat the same thing I always say to him?"

It doesn't have to be "bad blood" with a particular person. More often it's a bad blood topic. These can be like open sores, or the proverbial hornet's nest.

One such very touchy issue got fired up in Brooklyn not too long ago. It concerned a proposed upgrade to Fort Green Park. This park was long neglected when the city was down and out. Now, since the city is geared toward improvements, it finally turned its eye to this particular park. New York City's Department of Parks and Recreation announced that it was going to build a new entrance. By the time people heard about it, the blueprints had been created and it was too late for folks to weigh in. The plans involved a wide and very grand concrete entryway into the park, which necessitated taking down fifty mature trees and grassy mounds in the northwest corner. In the rendering of the plans the city posted, the entry was lined with rows of unnamed vendors. This is a neighborhood that has gentrified very quickly; historically there were mostly working class people living there, and there are still housing authority houses lining one side of the park. There was bound to be upset about the plans, and it immediately became a fight over whose park it is.

One faction said, "No one is considering the welfare of these working class people, and they need the trees! They won't be able to afford all these expensive new vendors. That part of the park is heavily utilized. This whole redo is just to make it fancy for the new condos, for the rich people." The other side responded with things like "Don't poor people deserve a real entrance, much nicer than what we have now? Park improvement should be for all neighborhoods. You just have a heart attack whenever there is change, and you are only complaining because you didn't get to see the blueprints beforehand." To complicate matters, the city tried to claim the trees were diseased anyway, which turned out to be somewhat false. One group filed a Freedom of Information Law request to get the correct information on the health of the trees. For all I know this fight will still be going on long after this book is published.

The point is this dispute became extremely bitter, especially online. On Nextdoor.com, for example—as well as on various listserves for people with kids—people who were normally well behaved were posting in all caps. According to my friend Sarah, who lives in this neighborhood, the ferocity of the opinions on this issue was incredible. And everyone was so sure the other side was coming from a bad place. There was a lot of ugliness.

This was one of those cases where it would not be obvious who was on each of the two "sides"; the opposing factions didn't really align along any readily apparent racial, political affiliation, or social class lines. During this time, if you went to a neighborhood party, you would absolutely *not* want to bring this subject up. Sarah said, "You just would never know when you would suddenly be faced with someone who was, just that afternoon, screaming angrily online." This is an example of a minefield you definitely do not want to step in, and unlike most minefields, this is one you *know* is there somewhere, lurking at every party held anywhere near this Brooklyn neighborhood.

According to Sarah, most people she knows in her area stay far away from this subject at get-togethers, as the debate about it is so vitriolic. But of course, it's always your choice whether or not you want to enter into an "open wound" topic. And obviously you can't control someone else bringing it up. Later in this book, I will describe ways to handle it if someone does bring up an explosive topic that you *do not* want to discuss.

Your assumptions are your windows on the world. Scrub them off every once in a while, or the light won't come in.

—Alan Alda

CHAPTER TWO

Safe Starts and Innocuous Initial Forays

If you have your mind unset and you know where many of your pitfalls lie, you've prepared yourself psychologically to enter the party. Remember that most of the time conversational minefields are just that—things you step in by accident. So you usually want to proceed gingerly, always being a little careful where you are stepping.

It can be helpful to take a moment to read the room. What is the body language of the other guests? Are people drunk and rowdy, or more subdued and relaxed? What is the reason for the social event, and what is its mood? How are people dressed? While I mostly discourage assuming things about people, there are often certain things you actually *can* surmise about a group as a whole. I hate to say it, but if everyone at the party is either dressed in Brooks Brothers suits or sporting Birkenstocks, you have an inkling of what kind of party you've walked into.

Always have a look around at your surroundings, like a good scientist, before diving into a room full of strangers. If you are not taken by surprise, you are more likely to be able to field anything that comes your way.

RULE NUMBER ONE...AND TWO AND THREE: NEVER ASSUME

As useful as it can be to have a sense of what the room is like, as far as whether it is conservative or liberal, young or old, urban or suburban, business or casual, try hard not to make too many assumptions about the beliefs and attitudes of the individual guests. Assuming is one of our worst human traits. This is a good rule whether you are mingling with the enemy or not—it's a life rule. Assumptions are the cause of many unnecessary conflicts, from marital spats to world wars.

One Republican I interviewed told me that whenever he is socializing with liberals (which he does often, as he is a writer living in Manhattan), he experiences "what we conservatives call 'virtue signaling'—which is their reminding me in no uncertain terms that I'm a bad person because I am a Republican and that they are morally superior because they are Democrats." The other side of the coin, of course, is conservatives presupposing that all liberals are self-righteous or overly politically correct, or "snowflakes."

So often our assumptions about people are wrong. One of the many people I have encountered who typify the idea of wrong assumptions is a friend of a friend named Tim. Tim is a cool-looking white man with shoulder-length hair who works as a drug rehabilitation counselor in Dallas. He's so progressive in his atti- tude about his clients that he advocates a drop-in center (where addicts can come in and have their drugs administered to them safely, without anyone passing judgment) and supports the use of acupuncture as part of rehab treatment. He has a master's degree in social work, and he loves to bake his own bread. He's married to a Mexican-American woman with whom he has a daughter.

Politically? Tim is a conservative, proudly pro-Trump, Rush Limbaugh-loving Republican.

Naturally most people would never suspect this. We have all gotten used to pigeonholing everyone into one rigid category or another. The truth is most people are complicated and have a variety of beliefs. This tendency to assume extends way beyond politics. I know of a woman who is petite with a bob haircut, dresses mostly in understated, neutral-colored cotton clothing, and wears no jewelry except pearl stud earrings. She's actually a professional jazz singer and drives a motorcycle. People used to assume that because I was single, over fifty, and had two cats, I did not like men or dogs. Guess what? I like both.

However, the main reason for avoiding assumptions has nothing to do with how erroneous they might be, but is more about the fact that your assumptions will actually impede the flow of conversation—first, because you may not hear what that person is actually saying if you are expecting them to have a certain opinion, and second, because people can sense your assumptions. Assumptions are almost like subtle, unspoken insults you convey to the other person.

Here's a quote from Martin Luther King, Jr. I always like to take with me into "enemy territory": "You have very little morally persuasive power with people who can feel your underlying contempt." When you make an assumption about someone based on five or ten minutes of conversation, and it's a negative assumption, it can sabotage the whole conversation. Liberals should not assume all conservatives are uncaring materialists or racists; conservatives should not assume all liberals are immoral, America-hating elitists.

AVOIDING THE THIRD RAIL: THE ABCS OF SOME COMMON VOLATILE TOPICS

The following list is obviously an oversimplification; most people already know what the potentially explosive subjects are. And of course, some people never shy away from any subject. In a perfect world we could all discuss these topics intelligently and not have the conversation deteriorate. Nevertheless, before you blunder ahead and "step in it," you might want to think twice—especially when you are not with people you know—before bringing up any of the following topics. While they can sometimes lead to an interesting discussion, they also might be the equivalent of a verbal hand grenade:

A is for Abortion

B is for Black Lives Matter

C is for Climate change

D is for Death penalty

E is for Economic inequality

F is for Financial regulation

G is for Gun control

H is for Health care

I is for Inheritance tax

J is for Jokes that can't be told anymore

K is for Kneeling, as in the taking of the knee

L is for "Liberal media"

M is for Marriage equality

N is for Nuclear nonproliferation

O is for Ozone layer

P is for Putin

Q is for Quotas

R is for Rain forest (disappearance of)

S is for Sexual harassment

T is for Trump

U is for Unions

V is for Vaccines

W is for the Wall

X is for Xenophobia

Y is for Yemen

Z is for Zero-tolerance policies

Note: No matter what subjects you choose to avoid, you really can never predict when you might accidentally set off a bombshell in casual conversation. A friend of mine who lives on Cape Cod was talking to a stranger, making what she thought was harmless small talk. She happened to mention to the person that she liked Tom Brady (as did the stranger) but that at the same time, she could understand how people outside of New England might not.

According to my friend, within minutes this person accused her of having a problem with excellence, not understanding the importance of working hard, and being a "typical liberal." My friend said she was really taken aback by this because she was actually saying she *liked* Brady; she was only trying to acknowledge that she knew there was some controversy surrounding him. The lesson is that you just never know when trying to engage in friendly banter can lead to bombs being thrown. (Of course, I, who do not follow football at all, had no idea what this melee was even about when my friend told me about it, though I did know Tom Brady was a football player. "Is he a quarterback?" I think I asked her. And I also know that admitting this ignorance on my part will, I'm sure, make someone else mad at *me!*)

SAFE DOESN'T HAVE TO MEAN BORING

If just about every single interesting and relevant topic seems too slippery a slope for the group you are in, what in the world *do* you talk about? What's the point if we are only chit chatting robotically about how bad the rush hour traffic was, how lovely the hostess looks, or how you've never before had guacamole that was quite this delicious?

For those times you are looking for subject matter, or you want to steer the conversation to nonpolitical areas, think of restaurants you've been to, places you've traveled to, sports you follow, books you've read (no political biographies, please), and of course, pets and children. Admittedly, these subjects do not always lead to fascinating repartee. And these days any subject is a potential minefield. But I have found if you want to have really fun discussions that are not political, they usually come from one of the following categories.

Personal Experience

In general, a good way to have real conversations with people while staying away from politics is to focus on experience rather than ideas. In other words, if someone mentions that they read in the news that Congress is voting on whether or not to raise the minimum wage, you can ask the person if they remember what their very first job was and how much they made an hour (rather than weighing in on the issue). That can give way to what that job experience was like, what your own first job was like, and so on. If someone remarks that the amount of snow we've gotten surely indicates something about global warming, you can ask the person if they grew up in an area that got snow and whether they remember how much fun playing in the snow was as a child. "Did you have a sled, or one of those saucers?" (I think the saucers are all plastic now; the metal ones were faster!)

The Offbeat Interview

Rather than asking other people where they live and what they do for a living, why not ask them more whimsical, nonthreatening questions—ones that can lead to abstract, creative conversation? For example, "Do you remember how old you were when you learned to tie your shoelaces?" That can lead to talk about how there are no shoelaces anymore, and who invented Velcro anyway? Or for that matter, who invented the zipper? Other kinds of offbeat questions include "What's the worst screw up in the kitchen you've ever had?" "Where is the most beautiful place you've ever been?" "Do you have a favorite number, and if so, why is it your favorite number?" Note: Most of these questions work best when you are talking with two or more people.

Tech Talk

Usually someone standing nearby will have a smartwatch or smart band on them or have their phone out, or perhaps Alexa is playing the music. This can be a lead-in to topics like the latest Apple product or the new wearable gadget everyone is talking about. This in turn can generate all kinds of interesting conversational meanderings, such as "Would you ever think about getting a chip inserted in your hand to replace your credit cards and I.D., which I hear is the next innovation coming?" Or "Did you know that Steve Jobs originally never foresaw iPhones as being such a big part of everyone's life, that he didn't think there would be a big market for them?" Or "Did you know there's a guy who's developing 3D smartphones?" Or "Did you know they've built robots that play ping-pong?" Or even, "Do you believe that whole brain emulation—the uploading of a human mind onto a computer—will ever be possible?"

Weird Science and Nature Subjects

At the risk of sounding like a trivia nerd, I often think the best conversations involve unusual or weird science stories, or interesting facts about nature. It's not a bad idea to have some of these tidbits at the ready. I once read a story about a biotech company in Montreal that was combining spider and goat DNA to create a unique milk, which was then used to make bullet-proof vest material. Once in a while I throw this story into the conversation, if people are talking about clothes or insects. (It also can be a way to derail an argument about gun control.) You obviously can't just start suddenly talking out of the blue about spiders and goats, but if you have enough of these odd-but-true stories, one of them is bound to fit into a conversation. It can be really fun. For instance, did you know there are flying squirrels that glow pink in the dark? Did you know there is a psychological disorder called boanthropy, in which a human believes themselves to be a cow? Or that the human nose can remember 50,000 different scents?

International Trivia

Since travel is a common topic in many circles, sometimes it can be interesting to introduce subjects that involve intriguing things in other countries. I'm not suggesting you try to study up on these before going to a party, but whenever you come across a story like this in the news, just store it away for a later mingle!

For example, there is a library in Norway called the Future Library that is accumulating books that have never been read, manuscripts from well-known authors that no one will be able to read until about 100 years from now. The project's aim is to collect an original work every year from 2014 to 2114, at which point they will be printed and published, using the 1,000 trees that were planted for that purpose. It's easy to bring this up if there are books on the shelves at the party. You simply introduce the topic with "I just learned about…" or "I just read about…" Another example in this category: The English philosopher Jeremy Bentham was taxidermied after his death; the result is called an "auto-icon" and is kept at University College London. Fun France fact? The Bibliotheque National in Paris is where Madame Curie's notebooks are stored—in lead-lined boxes because they are still radioactive.

Spacey Stuff

Astronomy and space topics are also fairly safe (unless you are talking to someone who believes the moon landing was a hoax, then I'm afraid you're in trouble), such as space travel, aliens and UFOs, the galaxy, string theory, the theory of relativity, shooting stars, and eclipses. And why is it again that Pluto isn't a planet? How about the fact that the last paper Stephen Hawkings wrote before he died was on how to escape from a black hole? Most people like to talk about the stars and the universe. These space topics seem to be mostly nonpartisan, maybe because they remind us that we are all Earthlings.

Netflix Your Muscles

When all else fails, don't forget about what takes up much of our waking reality: TV and movies. We are living in the "Golden Age of TV," and once you start talking *Game of Thrones, Stranger Things, Bull, Killing Eve,* or *This Is Us,* the conversation usually sails along. Even if the other person has not watched *your* favorite show, talking about your show will remind them about how passionate they are about *their* favorite show, and how you absolutely *must* watch it. Almost everyone is binge-watching something on Netflix, Amazon Prime, Hulu, HBO, or Showtime, and everyone has a show they love so much they want everyone to try it.

However, as we have all probably experienced, even conversations about TV can easily lead to politics. Shows like *Homeland, House of Cards,* and *The Handmaid's Tale* are all too relevant and political. Even discussions of *Game of Thrones* can lead to politics (e.g., the wall of the Night's Watch/the proposed US/Mexican border wall).

And you know what? Maybe that's okay. So far in this book I've been spending a lot of time talking about avoiding minefields and circumventing subjects. Now, it's time to see what happens when you decide to brave the battlefield and mix it up a bit with the enemy.

The true spirit of conversation consists in building on another man's observation, not overturning it.

—Edward G. Bulwer-Lytton

CHAPTER THREE

Entering the DMZ:
Taking Chances

So now you know how you can read the room, avoid assumptions, and find low-risk topics. But is playing it safe really all we want from our social experiences? After all, what would be the purpose of mixing with new people if we limited our dialogue to the utterly noncontroversial? Perhaps you might be feeling, in the face of what happened in the news that day, that to try to talk only about how much snow you got or what movie you saw would be inane.

Also, it's not really good for us to always repress our thoughts and feelings. Research has shown that having more meaningful conversations leads to increased well-being. In one study at the University of Arizona, students wore microphones on their shirt collars for four days to capture their conversations; the psychologists found that the happiest person had twice as many substantive conversations—and only one-third the amount of small talk—as the unhappiest person.[5] Even though interactions at a cocktail party and similar social events do tend to be brief and plentiful, it's still possible to have stimulating conversations—and sometimes that means not shying away from controversy. Truly connecting with one another is, after all, our goal. It's the very thing we are not doing enough when we spend all our free time scrolling through Facebook posts and Instagram pics.

The point is not that we need to completely avoid *talking* politics, but that we need to avoid *arguing* politics. You just need to take a few precautions before diving in. With a little practice, you'll become proficient at knowing when the conversational water is safe, and when it's not.

THE REWARDS OF RESPECTFUL DEBATE

Part of navigating minefields is being able to ascertain when you have a clear road ahead—that is, being pretty sure nothing will suddenly blow up in your face. If everyone in the conversation seems committed to staying relatively calm, it can be rewarding to debate an issue that is close to your heart.

In spite of the impediments created by our polarized realities, we need to keep talking to one another, and to try to listen to the other person's point of view—as alien as it might sometimes seem to us. Authentic communication is the only hope that we have for the future of our society. If only five percent of us had our minds opened to something we never considered before, that could be the tipping point that saves us from an all-out civil war. In any case, modern life is too closely connected with politics to avoid contentious subjects entirely. Almost all subjects tend to lead to politics or some kind of partisan issue, and just because we are having fun at a party does not mean we can, or should, turn off our brains. As Yale law professor and columnist Stephen Carter writes in his book *Civility*, "Civil dialogue over differences is democracy's true engine: we must disagree in order to debate, and we must debate in order to decide, and we must decide in order to move." We shouldn't keep our mouths shut all the time simply to avoid potential conflict.

On the other hand, neither do you want to dash headlong into violent arguments at a social event. I interviewed someone who admitted that at parties he sometimes can't help "baiting" people who he knows are on the opposite political side. Later, after his opponent has taken the bait and the atmosphere has become tense, he often regrets it. Even if you are one of those people who finds yelling at the top of your lungs invigorating and see yourself as a missionary for your cause, remember that in general this course of action will make the party uncomfortable—not just for the target of your anger, but also for the people around you. While I admit it can sometimes be fascinating to watch people fighting from a safe distance, the way many of us can't help slowing down on the highway to look at an accident, it's definitely not fun if you are the hostess.

Remember, choosing not to fight does not mean you have to compromise what you believe in. Be an activist, write letters, go to marches, call your senator daily. But it's not necessary to ruin a Super Bowl party because you feel the urge to fulminate at the top of your lungs. At social get-togethers you want discourse, not disaster, and there is a difference between a lively debate and a quarrel. Sometimes it can be a fine line to walk, but when you manage to do it, it can be immensely satisfying. The key is realizing that you don't have to—and that you probably won't be able to—convince the other person.

I met an unusual man at a party in Manhattan not too long ago, named Mitch. When I began to explain the book I was writing, his eyes lit up. "Ah!" he said, "whenever I meet someone at a party who I disagree with I relish the experience enormously."

"Huh?" was my stupefied response.

"Oh yes, I immediately go off to a corner with him if I can." Mitch, a fairly liberal Democrat, told me he finds it interesting, instructive, and challenging to talk to someone who is on the opposing side of an issue. He doesn't try to change the other person's mind; he doesn't need to win. He simply likes the exchange of information.

Mitch told me he had recently gone on a fishing trip out West with his teenage son. One gorgeous sunny day on the bank of the Yellowstone River, they found themselves fishing next to an older man, a native Montanan. After Mitch and the man had chatted a while about fishing, the older man brought up deer hunting and asked Mitch if he owned a gun. Mitch said he didn't, and asked the man what kind of gun he had. Among the several guns the older man owned was an AR-15. Now, this was only three weeks after the 2018 Florida school shooting, but Mitch managed to ask the man calmly, "But why the AR-15—what's it for?"

The man replied by asking Mitch if he had ever shot a gun, and Mitch said he had, once, when he was young. "Well," said the man, "you know that jolt you get when you pull the trigger, how pleasurable it is? Well, an AR-15 gives you fifteen of those great jolts one after the other."

After asking the man more questions about how and when he had first acquired this gun and what he used it for (to shoot at targets was the man's answer), Mitch ventured, "But what about all the people that particular type of gun has killed? Is that pleasure you get from those jolts really worth all those lives? Do you think this gun should be so readily available to everyone, just for recreation's sake?"

The man, bristling, muttered that of course crazy people shouldn't be able to have them, and then, raising his voice, started talking about the Second Amendment—about how it had been written into the Constitution to make sure that all Americans would be able to own guns.

"Well, we are certainly in agreement on guns and crazy people," Mitch said with a conciliatory smile. He could tell from the man's reaction that any further conversation about gun control would be useless. So he switched the subject back to tying flies and spoon casting.

Some people would have challenged the Montanan's position further, tried to argue with him—to make the point that ordinary citizens should not have military-style automatic weapons, and that the writers of the Second Amendment were referring to a state militia, and also never foresaw these kinds of guns. But this was a fishing vacation and a conversation with a local, not a town hall meeting. Mitch had enough delicacy, self-discipline, and savvy to know just how far to go in this conversation. He gained insight about another's point of view (he certainly had never heard anyone talk about the pleasurable jolts!), and even though he was upset by the man's defense of AR-15s, he did not fall over the edge into anger in a situation when having an argument would clearly not have done any good. He made his point and backed away.

I sometimes think of this as balance-beam socializing. Sometimes it's just interesting to see if you can do it. Like an exercise in restraint. Nothing is wrong with understanding how other people think; hearing other opinions will not actually hurt you (with the possible exception of out-and-out hate speak, but we'll get to that later). And sometimes the most interesting things can happen when you have a conversation about an issue with someone whose ideas are very different from yours. I remember years ago, when I was in my twenties, having a discussion with my conservative brother-in-law about the economy. We drank wine and debated. And even though once in a while I would feel my adrenaline rise, we didn't get truly angry. I can't remember exactly what we talked about (probably a dispute about the efficacy of small government versus the value of funding social services), but I remember the conversation was invigorating and made me feel better than if I had dodged the subject just because we disagreed. It made me feel very alive, the way you do when you dance the tango or play racquetball.

One of my favorite Malcolm Gladwell quotes is this one: "Look at the world around you. It may seem like an immovable, implacable place. It is not. With the slightest push—in just the right place—it can be tipped." Everything is worth discussing; there's always a chance you could open another person's mind, just a millimeter, if you are brave enough to enter into this potentially combustive territory. For example, I used to be adamantly against all hunting, until one day when I dared to voice this viewpoint to a duck-hunting acquaintance. Over the next half hour, he succeeded in pointing out to me the hypocrisy of my loving to eat a duck but being squeamish about being a part of its death. Later he sent me an article on the horrible conditions of most duck farms, an article that almost turned me into a vegetarian. I never complained about duck hunting again.

There is an amazing man who I believe epitomizes the art of respectful debate: Daryl Davis, the subject of a documentary called *Accidental Courtesy*. The first time I heard him interviewed was on the podcast "Love and Radio." A musician, author, and public speaker, Davis is a black man who has spent years befriending members of the Ku Klux Klan; he sits down with these white supremacists/separatists and lets them air their views. He politely asks them questions—challenging ones—about why they believe what they believe. At first they are suspicious and defensive, but eventually, they begin to ask him questions in return. Most people could not show the restraint Davis does in the face of the hateful things they say. But he allows them to express their views; when he disagrees, he tells them so, but in such a way that they do not feel attacked. After many years of Davis's building these relationships, many of these Klan members have completely renounced their affiliation with the Klan. They have surrendered their KKK robes to Davis as a tribute to their friendship. In almost every interview he gives, Davis says the important thing he learned was this: "While you are actively learning about someone else, you are passively teaching them about yourself." He believes that you don't have to respect what others are saying, but you must respect their right to say it—and that often they will then afford the same courtesy to you.

CONVERSATIONAL RECON: HOW TO TEST FOR FRIENDS, FOES, OR FANATICS

However, not all of us are ultra-patient crusaders like Mr. Davis, and even he would not be able to achieve much in one twenty-minute conversation. At a party, especially if it is a business-related event, often the best thing to do—should you feel that the conversation is leading to a controversial topic, or you have the urge to bring one up yourself—is to probe the mood and disposition of your conversational partner. Like having a good radar detector, there are ways to tell in advance if you are entering an emotionally toxic area. One effective strategy is to throw out a trial question or comment and judge by the other person's response whether it's a good idea to proceed. In this manner, you can test for "friend, foe, or fanatic."

For our purposes here, a "friend" is someone who feels the way you do about an issue. A "foe" is someone who is on the opposite side of an issue but is still open-minded, or at least able to hear you out. A "fanatic" is someone (usually, but not always, on the opposite side) whose opinions are set in stone and are completely black and white—and who is very easily angered and itching for a fight. An important thing to keep in mind is that these questions are not just for discerning whether the person holds an opposing view. They are designed to gauge something more important: the basic temperament of the person. A fanatic who is on your side of an issue but who is unyielding, pedantic, and super-radical can be just as difficult and exhausting as a fanatic from the other side. Personally, I'd almost rather talk to a reasonable, middle of the road "foe" than someone who voted the way I did but thinks every single person who voted for the other candidate is the devil incarnate.

Denver clinical psychologist Susan Heitler offers this warning about these kinds of ideologues on her popular *Psychology Today* blog: "It's no fun talking politics to someone who is certain he has all the right answers. As beliefs consolidate into sets of ideas bounded by impenetrable walls, there will be increasingly little uptake of non-confirmatory data, that is, ideas that differ from what he already believes. A fixed system of beliefs that allows for no additional data to enter is clinically termed a delusional system." Again, I'm *not* talking here about people who simply have extreme political views. Some of my own friends fall into this category and can still keep their cool when they are at parties. The kind of fanatics I refer to here have angry conversations about the issues going on inside their heads all the time. They are often primed by recent fights with friends and family, or by something they've read in the news or seen in a rant on TV—or in those inflammatory tweets that are always flying around nipping at our psyches (so unlike the soothing sounds of real birds!). They are absolutists, and usually exceedingly self-righteous. So when an offhand comment is made, this kind of fanatic immediately infers context and meaning that is often not actually there. In addition, the fanatic has been storing up brilliant ways to make his point since the last time the issue was broached. It's like a Pavlovian response. The fanatic is often not really listening to what's being said in the present moment.

The following test lines may help you spot this kind of fanatic before it's too late. They are designed as an early warning system to let you know if you are talking to someone who is likely to quickly become belligerent; the person's reaction will help you decide whether or not you can have a civilized conversation. Finding the right moment for your test question, so it doesn't seem to come out of nowhere, is crucial. Keep a close watch on facial expressions and body language when you administer the test.

Note: The test lines below are only suggestions, and some of the responses are somewhat exaggerated in order to make my point. Naturally this testing device requires your own personal touch. Also know that these kinds of tests are never foolproof. People's belief systems are not always as straightforward as you expect them to be.

Sample test lines:

* "I think I just saw someone who looks like _____ [e.g., Hillary Clinton/Mike Pence/Elizabeth Warren/Ted Cruz/ Michael Moore/Sean Hannity]." Note: Don't use an obvious person like Trump, whose looks have been the butt of so many jokes. It won't be an effective test.

Examples of fanatical responses:

"If it was him, I hope you hurt him."

"I feel sorry for anyone who looks like her."

* "I always wonder why they use blue for Democrats and red for Republicans. How did that come about?"

  Examples of fanatical responses:

  "Blue must be because of all the stupid crying and whining the liberals do."

  "Maybe red is for all the blood on their hands."

* "I was watching the news last night on _____ [e.g., MSNBC/Fox News]."

  Examples of fanatical responses:

  "I wouldn't really call that news. More like propaganda if you ask me."

  "So I assume that's the only place you ever get your news?"

* "The weather sure has been crazy recently."

  Examples of fanatical responses:

  "I hope you are not one of those global warming freaks. That's just a left-wing conspiracy, you know."

  "Yes, we can thank the oil companies for our dying planet."

TELLTALE WARNING SIGNS OF IMPENDING CONVERSATIONAL DOOM

Of course, the trouble with being a conversational adventurer is that if you're not careful you can suddenly find yourself right smack in the middle of extreme discomfort. I still cringe about the time many years ago I was holding forth with a doorman about how mean the building super was. After a few minutes I began to notice that the doorman, usually quite friendly and talkative, wasn't saying much. I paused, and finally, he said, "You know the super is my father, don't you?"

Although this was not a political conversation, it is a good example of how important it is to pick up on cues. If I had been more engaged in the conversation and watching the doorman more carefully, I would probably have noticed something was awry sooner from his expression.

I interviewed someone, a woman named Margie, who told me of an embarrassing conversation she ended up in, mostly because she had not been paying attention to her audience. She was recounting a story her aunt had told her, about the time a "bunch of gypsies" robbed her house. Supposedly, a woman had rung the doorbell and when the aunt answered the door, several little children who had been hiding under the woman's full skirt scattered throughout the house. Margie, who was only telling the story as an example of how her aunt tended to exaggerate, never noticed that the person she was talking to had grown very uncomfortable at the use of the term "bunch of gypsies." The person was quite offended and gave Margie a lecture on the disparaging nature of the term "gypsy," which Margie, after years of hearing her aunt tell the story, had not even thought about. (She definitely knows better now.)

So how do you know whether you are being interesting or are about to fall into the pit of someone's intense disapproval? If you are both smiling, if no one is yelling, and if no one seems terribly uncomfortable, you are probably okay. But do a self-check: Are you still listening to the other person's words, or are you just waiting to pithily propel your next point into the air? Is the other person shaking their head or rolling their eyes? Usually you can spot the warning signs if you are paying attention at all. And these days it's even more important to be paying attention. Here are some tips:

* **Notice any strange or sudden silences.** There are many reasons to stay attuned to the other person's reactions. But paying attention is especially important when you are beginning to touch on a potentially dangerous subject. Let's say you've administered a test question and are pretty sure you are not talking to a fanatic, so you launch into one of your favorite subjects about how a particular senator is self-serving, or how you think the latest Supreme Court decision is a disaster. After a bit, you happen to notice, when you pause for a reaction, that the other person is just staring at you, or nodding slightly without smiling. Maybe their eyes are shifting around nervously, or they start fidgeting. These are signs your conversation may be about to get sticky. It may be best to pivot to another topic.

* **Listen for the following advance warning phrases (not all these necessarily mean trouble, but look alive!):**

  "Hmm, I don't know about that."

  "Right, that's what a lot of people think."

"You seem rather passionate about this."

"Ah. So you're one of *those* people."

"Sometimes I get so tired of stuff like this."

"Do people really still believe that?"

"I guess I don't really get the joke."

DON'T BE A KNEE JERK: TECHNIQUES FOR AVOIDING OVERREACTION

Few of us ever think of ourselves as being fanatical or dogmatic. (Who, me?) So let's agree: I've certainly never been unduly opinionated, and neither have you, dear reader. We also never bounced a check, got a parking ticket, or lied about our age or our weight.

Let's face it, we are all human, and once in a while every one of us can react in a way that is unconstructive or even rude. Maybe you've had a bad day. Perhaps someone just happened to hit your rawest nerve. Or maybe one of your test questions backfired and the other person has uttered something truly offensive. These can be tough moments. To begin with, you have to acknowledge that there are times when we ourselves are guilty of overreacting. Saying, "I do not agree with you about that at all" may be a conversation stopper but is not necessarily an overreaction. However, something like "Well *that's* what's wrong with our country right there. Misinformed people like you who are fucking everything up!" is.

Please note: I am NOT saying that you should not have strong opinions, and that you are not in some sense "right" to feel moved by the spirit of justice or the desire to be heard. But if you are angry, at least some of what you are feeling is fear. Remember, there are people who benefit from dividing us, and they use fear to do it. So in a way it might help you to think, *If I overreact, the terrorists win!*

The following techniques are for those times when you feel impelled to say something in anger—something unkind or accusatory. After you have squelched your overreaction, after you have headed off your anger at the pass, you can then employ one of the subject-changing or escape strategies I'll demonstrate in later chapters. (With all of the techniques below, you need to take a big breath or two first. They are all creative versions of counting to ten.)

Consult Your Inner Psychic: Predict the Future (of This Conversation)

Let's say you've just been talking about something you think of as fairly trivial when suddenly the person you're speaking with seems to be implying that you are a sexist and an anti-feminist, or a mushy-minded liberal dupe. You feel your hurt and anger rise. While you are taking your calming breath, quickly follow the conversation to its inevitable conclusion in your mind—that is, what the other person is likely to say back if you were to respond with the defensive, angry comment that's come to mind. As if it were a chess game, try to see four or five moves ahead before you speak. You've been here before, you've had this kind of conversation. You know what will happen. Is it worth it?

Practice Astral Projection: Leave Your Body

I realize most therapists and mindfulness coaches will tell you that mental and spiritual health is all about staying in your body.

But hey, we are not all spiritual masters. There are times when you may have to check out, just for a second or two, to keep from exploding. So when you feel your own inner volcano starting to roil, picture yourself floating up to the ceiling, for just a moment, like a fish swimming to the surface of the water to get more oxygen. After a moment you can come back down and reenter your body. (Reentry is obviously a must.) You can also, of course, transport yourself to your "happy place"—envision that you are at your favorite beach, river, or mountaintop. A more prosaic version of this technique is to think about what you are going to cook for dinner tomorrow, or what you are planning to wear to work.

Channel Mr. Spock

You are chatting away happily when all at once you find the other person is praising the actions of a public figure you absolutely despise. If you want to live long and prosper at this party, think about how Spock would react. He would probably say, "Fascinating," while raising his eyebrow. Or "That is quite interesting." Whatever he would say, he would say it serenely, as a scientist who is studying this crazy human race. (Warning: Do not stay in Spock mode for too long. Too much Vulcan can be decidedly off-putting.)

Stuff Your Face

Fill your mouth with food. As quickly as possible, before you say something you regret. I say food, not drink, because keeping anger in check is not easy if you over-imbibe, and also a mouthful of liquid takes less time to swallow than food. By the time you get done chewing, you will have reconsidered the harsh retort that was rising to your lips. Bread is excellent for this, especially if it's dry. While you are chewing, you can nod or shake your head in response to what the other person is saying, but that's about all.

You may end up gaining weight using this one, if you are someone who has a short fuse. Try to stay close to the raw vegetables!

While the strategies covered in this chapter are easy to employ and can be quite useful and effective, there are other, more organic ways of dealing with mingling with the enemy. However, be forewarned. In the next chapter, I may be using a four-letter word that could offend some people: love.

The opposite of hate is the beautiful and powerful reality of how we are all fundamentally linked and equal as human beings. The opposite of hate is connection.

—Sally Kohn

CHAPTER FOUR

The Way of the Empath

The word "empath" does not have exactly the same connotation as "empathy." An empath is someone who is able to understand or feel the emotions of another. On the other hand, "empathy" implies being able to *share* those emotions. In this chapter, I'm talking more about understanding or "feeling the person" than being in agreement or sharing the same views. (For instance, if you run into someone at a party who is projecting hate or fear, you obviously don't want to "share" that feeling.) The main idea of the way of the empath is to try to have compassion for people, with all their human flaws—even when you disagree with them intellectually, or even morally or ethically.

I had the opportunity to speak about the concept of mingling with "the enemy" with Schuyler Vogel, Senior Minister of the Universalist Unitarian (UU) church in New York City, who holds degrees in religion from Carleton College and Harvard Divinity School. Reverend Vogel believes deeply in the first principle of the UU church: the inherent worth and dignity of every individual. "Having compassion for people on the other side is hard," he said. "It takes willpower. For UUs, our first principle extends across all things; you don't get to decide who gets to have that or not. Part of it is reminding ourselves to have humility, to remember that human experience is vast and unpredictable and unknowable to any one person. And that there are undoubtedly experiences and perspectives that we can not understand, but they are very real to another human being."

"I think part of the role of a minister, but also the role of good, emotionally mature people—and that goes for minglers as well—is to try to understand the emotional needs of people you are with," he told me. "And if you can, address them. Or at least be attuned to them in a way that's kind. I think a lot of times when people get really mad during an argument, they're feeling really insecure and in danger of being judged themselves. They feel like their humanity, if they lose that argument, is somehow diminished."

Trying to act on this idea is a whole lot easier said than done. One of the hardest things to deal with is standing across from someone who has just said something that you disagree with so much it takes your breath away, or someone who is suddenly very angry at something that you said. Choosing the way of the empath can be difficult, but it can also be powerful and rewarding. In general, it's all about forcing yourself to see the other person as a valuable fellow human. Part of how you do this is training yourself to be a better listener, and learning how to be as giving as possible whenever you find yourself conversing with the enemy. Being generous, flexible, and loving in conversation is not always doable, but it's a goal to strive for. Surprising things can happen when you succeed even partially.

LISTEN WITH ALL YOUR MIGHT (THEN LISTEN SOME MORE)

It's challenging enough under normal circumstances to be a good listener. Many of us have trouble with this skill, especially during those times when we are socializing with a lot of people together in one place. This is usually not because we are egotistical or narcissistic, although that can sometimes be the case. Mostly it's because we are nervous, distracted, or just plain lazy.

Perhaps we have just heard the other person say something that we don't quite understand, so instead of listening to what they are saying now, our minds begin racing, trying to figure it out. Or we could be only half listening because we are terrified that we are going to be caught not remembering someone's name, or afraid that we have lettuce in our teeth or stains on our ties. Sometimes we are tired and hungry or stressed out and don't have the patience to listen well. Other times we think we have the perfect thing to say and are concerned we won't have time to get it into the conversation, so we are just waiting for our turn to talk instead of really listening. We are often too focused on appearing smart or interesting when, ironically, the most successful minglers are master listeners, people who talk 50 percent or less during a conversation.

The key is to listen with your whole being. Listen to the other person with both your ears and your mind. Engage the whole brain, rather than using part of it for something else, which we all tend to do. We often think, *I can listen to this man speak and still make a plan for what I am going to have for dinner tomorrow; after all, he's not speaking that quickly.*

Also, you need to pay attention not just to the words but to all the other signals; you need to listen *between the lines.* Listen to the words coming out of the person's mouth, but also listen for what is behind those words. Pay attention to facial expressions and other body language. What part of this conversation is having an effect on the other person? What do they smile at, what makes them look away? Try to see what's behind the words; ask yourself, *What is the motivation behind these thoughts? What is this person thinking?* Stay in the present moment. And listen at least as much as you talk.

Obviously a part of your mind is going to form responses during the conversation, but try to keep your response in the back of your mind until it seems the other person wants or needs a response. When you do respond, it helps to repeat some of what they have just said in your response, as that shows the person you've really been listening. However, do resist the temptation to finish other people's sentences. This particular kind of jumping in may seem like a method for bonding with the other person conversationally, as if you are saying, "Yes, I really understand you," but any type of interruption is usually quite jarring to the other person. (Moreover, there is always the chance you will complete their sentence incorrectly, and that can be truly annoying.) The truly empathetic listener is quiet, and follows rather than trying to lead, encouraging the speaker to elucidate.

Now, all this is a hundred times tougher when what the other person is talking about is setting your teeth on edge. Still, endeavor to let them have their say. It's not going to kill you, even though it feels like it might. And sometimes when a person feels heard, they will not have the need to make their point with anger. The result can be a more rational conversation.

ASK REAL QUESTIONS

Everyone likes to feel that others are interested in what they think and feel. Asking questions is an important part of any mingling experience. Try to be curious; be inquisitive. Be an information gatherer. In situations where you are mingling with the enemy, one way to keep from losing your temper is to ask questions in lieu of reacting negatively to what the person is saying. If you are feeling provoked by something that has been said, this kind of "tell me more" strategy may help keep your emotions in check, at least momentarily. This is similar to the strategy of stuffing your face with food that I described in chapter three. Better to listen a little more than to end up insulting another person. It will give you time to formulate your response, so that if you do want to then counter what they are saying, it will come out better.

Try not to ask defensive questions or questions that are really statements in disguise. We see lawyers use these kinds of questions all the time. For example, don't say, "Since you are a conservative, I bet you believe such-and-such about this and that, right?" Instead, be sure to phrase it this way: "What do you think about this and that?"

Don't ask yes or no questions; ask questions that invite the other person to talk at length. The best kinds of questions are ones in which you also share something about yourself. This encourages the other person to open up. For example, "I grew up in a suburb of Chicago and didn't really see much of urban life until I was out of college. Where did you grow up?"

If what the person is saying is too hard for you to listen to, you can always change the subject or leave the person using one of the techniques illustrated later in this book. However, first try to really understand who the person is, what they're all about. And if it's outlandishly wacky stuff that's coming out of their mouth, tell yourself that you can use the material as entertainment in your next discussion with a close friend on the same subject.

VISUALIZATION: PICTURING THE INNER THREE-YEAR-OLD

This is a little trick I invented (though I'm sure I'm not the first to think of it) while I was sitting on the subway one day at rush hour, tired and disgusted with the behavior of my fellow humans. There were the usual boneheaded people blocking the doorway, impeding people from getting on or off. Across from me there was a classic manspreader, sprawling his legs out in a huge V and taking up way too much room on this very crowded train. One woman near me was loudly talking away, oblivious to the fact that she was letting her bag, which was hanging from her shoulder, bump gently but rhythmically into someone else's head. I looked at everyone and took a breath, aware that my negative feelings about my fellow riders were making the ride more unpleasant for me. I closed my eyes. Telling myself to stop being so judgmental, I began to imagine everyone on the subway car as three-year-olds. Tired, hungry, fussy three-year-olds. Their little feet swinging, dangling off the floor. *Awww.* The poor little darlings were just trying to get through the ride home. I found myself smiling.

This is a good trick to use at a party, should you suddenly find yourself surrounded by people spouting upsetting views, things you find too ugly to debate. *Look at all these fussy three-years-olds,* you can say to yourself. *They all must be up past their bedtime.*

LOVE AND FLATTERY ARE YOUR BEST FRIENDS; KEEP THEM CLOSE

Flattery, like small talk, has gotten a bad rep. It is not necessarily superficial and insincere. At least not the kind I'm talking about. Instead of thinking about spewing out compliments, think of it as giving out love, or positive energy. I am not suggesting you compliment someone on a point of view or opinion you disagree with. The idea is to flatter them before there is any serious talk.

For example, let's say you are introduced to Carlos, who is a friend of Bob, the host. If applicable, you might immediately say, "Oh, you're Carlos? I've heard wonderful things about you from Bob! So great to meet you!" If someone has brought food to the party, make sure to mention in conversation that (1) it looks great, (2) it tastes fabulous (if you've had a chance to have some), or (3) it happens to be one of your very favorite things. If the person you are talking to is wearing glasses, a scarf, a hat, a pin, a tie, or a cool watch, tell them how much you like their accessory. Ask them where they got it. When flattering, you don't have to necessarily lie, just look for anything you can say something positive about.

Almost everyone responds well to compliments, especially if they seem genuine. People will warm up to you; they will like you for it. The National Institute for Physiological Sciences in Japan conducted a study in 2012 to measure the effect of receiving a compliment and found it to be equal to the effect of receiving cash.[6] Once people like you, they will be more open to other things you say, and it will be a little harder to get mad at you during the ensuing back and forth you may have on the current state of the union.

Some basic flattery no-no's: It's usually fine for women to compliment other women's clothing or shoes; however, for obvious reasons, in general men should not praise women's clothing or body shape—men should stick to accessories like glasses or hats. Don't use a compliment that is obviously insincere ("I've never met anyone as smart as you!") and don't offer self-serving compliments ("Bob told me that you're just like me—that you're *also* the life of the party!").

Remember, by emitting positive energy you are weeding the fear and anger out of a situation so that the ground will be fertile for a successful conversation. When you give someone positive energy, you are more likely to get similar energy back in return. This can elevate the conversation you will be having, even if you disagree with each other on the issues.

So hit them with your love ray. Not to sound too much like Oprah or anything, but love is actually the greatest weapon.

YIELDING WITHOUT LOSING: APPLYING TAI CHI PRINCIPLES IN CONVERSATION

My friend David called me up one morning to tell me about something upsetting that had happened to him the night before at a colleague's housewarming party. David didn't know many people there, and at one point he started chatting with a man and a woman, when suddenly there was an awkward silence. (A really bad one, he told me, one of those that seem to last forever.) Desperate to fill the void, David happened to notice that the song playing in the background was "Baby, It's Cold Outside." This had been one of his father's favorite Johnny Mercer records, and mostly because he couldn't think of anything else, he said, "Oh, I love this song."

Immediately he got a very cold stare from the woman. It almost knocked him over. "That's a song about date rape, you know," she snapped. "It should be banned." David said he was stunned, because just before they had all been talking about their various summer vacation plans and everything had been amiable.

He ended up just mumbling, "Sorry," and walking away. He felt so horrible after that, he just went home.

David felt it was a harmless comment, even though in retrospect he could see how the lyrics (he went back and listened to all of them on YouTube) might be a problem for people. But the woman had a point, of course. The song's lighthearted treatment of a situation that today could be viewed as sexual entrapment helps keep the "no means yes" mindset alive. And just because the music is romantic and the singers seem to be flirting doesn't mean it doesn't reflect centuries of inculcated sexism. On the other hand, several feminists have recently pointed out that if you listen to the lyrics closely, it's apparent that the woman really does want to give herself permission to stay the night, that she's fighting against the morality of that era, and that the idea that she could actually choose to have sex with the guy was revolutionary in its time. And let's not forget the song was written seventy-five years ago.

There is a whole genre of things written in the past—Doris Day movies, 50s musicals, Nabokov novels—that would (and should) be considered horribly offensive if they were created today. One could argue that these things are part of our cultural history and should be taken with a grain of contextual salt. Frank Loesser wrote "Baby, It's Cold Outside" in 1944 for him and his wife, Lynn Garland, to perform at parties in New York City. Loesser sold the song to MGM for a movie called *Neptune's Daughter*, and in this movie, the last half of the duet actually features a woman trying to seduce a man. (Lady Gaga and Tony Bennett reclaimed the song brilliantly by also switching the "cat" and "mouse" roles in their 2015 rendition.)

Why am I going into all this? Because this is the kind of detailed dialogue people *could* have about this song. The problem with the above party scenario is not the woman's opinion, but the way she expressed it. This is the kind of issue that people might even change their mind about, after they consider all the facts, but once David felt under attack that was never going to happen. From the way the woman responded to David's innocent comment, she was not open to discussing this topic on an intellectual level. He ran away partially because he was afraid the conversation was going to escalate unpleasantly.

If only one or both of the protagonists in this incident could have employed the principles of tai chi during this conversation.

Tai chi is a spiritual practice and martial art that draws on the idea of softness, of being relaxed. In fact, one of the things my tai chi teacher always used to tell the class was that we needed to "walk like a cat." A large part of learning to mingle well has to do with overcoming fear, just as the basis of tai chi is to let go of tension in the body. Hardness and resistance are the only real obstacles to success when you're mingling with the enemy. When you come up against something that feels like an attack, if you can remember to employ this important yielding principle, it will serve you well. The idea is that when someone pushes you, don't push back. Be soft; sink down into your center and stay relaxed. It's important to make a distinction here—this is not a "surrender," as in surrendering your viewpoint in an argument. It's almost as though you use the other person's force against them; you bend but never break. Picture those *wuxia* martial arts movies where your body can move away from the blows more quickly than they can land. In your mind you are secure in what you believe, even as you outwardly bend or yield. Applied to each of the participants in the interaction above, it would look something like this:

David would quickly realize the woman is not attacking him personally, she's just predisposed to react that way to this song.

First he would acknowledge what the woman has said. "Oh! I sure didn't mean to offend you. I guess I can see the reason for that kind of interpretation." Then he would employ a gentle counter-response like "It's such a familiar old tune I sometimes don't even think of the words. I don't think I even *know* all the words. But I appreciate your telling me how you feel. I'm not sure I agree with you, but I'm certainly open to giving it some thought."

Now, if the woman were suddenly able to also switch into tai chi mode, she might then respond, "Yes, thank you, it is worth examining. I realize it's a Christmas standard, and the music is nice, but the words are insidious. All these old seduction scenes we've grown up on are buried deep in our psyches and really do help keep the sexism status quo alive. I appreciate your willingness to rethink it."

At which point David might say, "And I really will. However, I just have to say that I wouldn't like the song so much if I did not get the feeling when I hear it that the woman is in love with the man and *wants* to spend the night. I wouldn't like it if I thought there was anything nonconsensual about it. I think they are both on the same page and having fun."

And the woman, still yielding without losing, would say something like "Well that's good to hear you say, David. Mostly all we can do is try to make sure we are looking at things clearly. But my point is men *always* think the woman is saying yes."

And so on. No resistance, strength through yielding. As Bruce Lee once wrote, "The strongest is he that makes use of his opponent's strength—be the bamboo tree which bends toward the wind; and when the wind ceases, it springs back stronger than before."

To argue with a person who has renounced the use of reason is like administering medicine to the dead.

—Thomas Paine

CHAPTER FIVE

Creative Survival Strategies

Sometimes no amount of empathy, flattery, or tai chi training can get you through the party when you are mingling with the enemy. Either you are simply not equal to talking about anything controversial that night, or you're up against someone you really don't feel like debating with. Even worse, it could be a case of your encountering excessive hostility while conversing with colleagues at the office, or an office social function. This is an ever-increasing problem. According to a recent study by Randstad USA, 64 percent of US employees say political discussions at work have grown more heated over the past five to ten years.[7] And if there's anywhere you don't want to have an ugly political argument, it's at work.

In these incendiary times, it's helpful to have some creative survival tricks up your sleeve, to either put out the fire or make it burn the way you want. Like all good minglers, you should not be above using a little fancy footwork to save yourself—and the situation.

STORYTELLING AS A SMOOTHING-OVER TECHNIQUE

A while ago a friend of mine, Samantha, attended a buffet lunch to celebrate the high school graduation of her friend's daughter, Kaya. She sat down on the couch next to a woman she didn't know, as it was the only seat left in the room at that point. Their conversation first centered around the graduation ceremony, then led to the subject of education in general. Samantha mentioned to the woman that she was a member of a charter school advocacy group and that they were hoping to open a new charter school in the area.

According to Samantha, the other woman became so incensed that she dropped her fork (which landed on the rug, leaving a smear of macaroni and cheese). The woman argued that charters pilfer money and students from district schools, that they aren't held accountable to anyone, and that it was a way of essentially privatizing public education. As her voice rose, she went on to say that charter schools were a "gateway drug" that would lead to more vouchers for private schools, and that they only served to discourage the government from focusing on public education reform the way it should.

Samantha tried in vain to get her own point of view across, to say that charter schools were subject to many of the same rules that govern traditional public schools and that numerous studies have found that the presence of charter schools had actually improved student achievement at nearby traditional public schools. Also, that especially in urban areas, students from low-income families thrived in charter schools. However, the woman kept getting more and more vociferous, and the discussion was becoming way too heated. So Samantha switched into storytelling mode.

First, Samantha transitioned from the topic by saying, "It's definitely a complicated issue. But getting back to Kaya, did I ever tell you about the time she and my daughter decided to make us all a five-course dinner, and almost burned the house down?" And without pausing she went on to recount the long, involved true story about the incident, complete with a description of the entire menu and the final blackened state of the potholder and apron, which had both caught on fire.

To be sure, for this survival technique to work you have to have a couple of appropriate stories at the ready. And sometimes when you feel you are under attack it can be hard to think of a good enough (or more important, long enough) story. I try to have in my mind one or two general party stories I could transition to, ones that will work in many different circumstances.

Side note: Be aware that when you are sitting, it can be very hard to physically escape an enemy. Getting up from a seat is not the same as slipping subtly away when you are both standing.

CONVERSATIONAL CAMOUFLAGING: HOW GOING UNDERCOVER IS SOMETIMES BETTER THAN WEARING YOUR OPINION ON YOUR SLEEVE

Sometimes it's not advantageous to show your true colors at the onset. I have found that going undercover sometimes garners the best results as far as getting my point across in the end. If I let a staunch conservative know right away that I am on the liberal side of an issue, they will often size me up as a "typical" East Coast Democrat and respond defensively right away. When coming up against their opposite, most people have a natural tendency to be more reactive, more self-justifying—to stick even more resolutely to their point of view.

The idea behind the conversational camouflage strategy is that you shift toward the other's viewpoint in order to connect with them (otherwise, they won't listen to you at all and will reject your ideas right away) and then, ideally, pull them gently back toward your position. It's a little bit sly, since you are, in a way, misrepresenting yourself—just in the beginning. But it often works a lot better than if you started out proselytizing. People will tend to drop their guard.

Here's an example. Let's say you are someone who is vehemently against fracking. You begin chatting with someone who you can tell from the start is totally pro-fracking. Here's the hypothetical conversation, with you in "conversational camouflage":

HIM: I just can't stand these people who go on about the dangers of fracking. My brother lives in North Dakota, and it's been so good for the economy there. It's a great, efficient source of natural gas. Without it we'd have to burn more coal. Then everyone would complain about *that*.

YOU: Right, a lot of people just don't see the whole picture.

HIM: (*more calmly, now that he believes you are not the enemy*) I mean, there's no such thing as clean energy. Every energy-procuring process has its risks.

YOU: Yeah. I have heard that fracking sometimes causes earthquakes. But I think they are usually just small ones. But anyway we definitely need energy sources that we don't have to import from another country.

HIM: Right. I mean, a lot of people are so against fracking, and they're protesting all over the place, but you better believe they still like to have fuel to heat their homes in the winter.

YOU: That's for sure. Though there are a lot of claims about the health problems people are having who live around the fracking sites. I hate to admit it but they actually seem pretty authentic. And some of those videos of people setting fire to the water in their kitchen sink are scary. Have you seen those? It's a little worrisome.

HIM: Well, I don't know if there's any real proof...

YOU: I just wish they could use chemicals that didn't cause cancer and birth defects.

HIM: I don't think...

YOU: All in all, when you think about it, with all the ingenuity in this country, with so many people developing things like space-based solar power, wind power, tidal power, you'd think we could find something less harmful to people and to the planet than fracking. Right?

THE POWER OF SILENCE

Many years ago, I attended a sales training seminar (though I can no longer remember what it was for or why I was there). Only one sales technique from that workshop has stuck with me: the "Pause Close." The idea of the Pause Close is that when trying to sell someone something, especially on the phone, at a certain point you just stop talking. Totally. You're supposed to say something to the other person and then sit there in complete silence, no matter what the other person says. Silence makes most people so uncomfortable that they are compelled to keep talking to fill the void. This was how you would get them to say yes to what you were selling. (After which, of course, you would begin speaking again!)

I rediscovered the technique about a year ago, when I was at a multigenerational party of a friend. It was a New Year's Day brunch, and I was one of only a few nonfamily guests invited, as I am very close friends with the hostess. There were about twenty people there—including some older in-laws and a couple cousins.

I was sitting in a circle of three or four people, sipping Bloody Marys, when the conversation turned to the origin of the name of the drink. In the midst of the talk about Mary Tudor—the English queen from whom the drink's name supposedly originated—one of the older in-laws, a man about seventy-five years old, brought up the character "Bloody Mary" from Rodgers and Hammerstein's musical *South Pacific* and made a racist comment. (In the story, Bloody Mary is Vietnamese but is often played by a black actress.) I won't repeat the remark here, but it was uttered as a joke, and was utterly unfunny. I think one or two people sitting in our circle might have pretended to laugh. The man was sitting across from me and was looking at me when he made the remark; previously I had been laughing at things he had been saying, and he therefore assumed I was a receptive audience.

I was shocked. A part of me wanted to chastise him, to call him out and tell him he was being racist. However, I did not feel it would be either appropriate or constructive to try to do so in this intimate gathering of my friend's family. On the other hand, neither did I want to indicate in any way that that kind of remark was okay. So I just very pointedly did not laugh. I kept my eyes straight ahead, averted from his, and said nothing. After an awkward silence he prodded me teasingly with, "I guess maybe some folks might think that was offensive." Again, I said nothing at all.

There is a reason they call it "the silent treatment." Silence is very powerful. As Che Guevara once said, "Silence is argument carried out by other means." I could tell that my silence embarrassed this man. I have a feeling he will hesitate before he makes a remark like that again. And yet, I did not humiliate him in the midst of his family, or ruin my friend's party by making it into a big noisy controversy. Believe me, the man got the point. With silence you can sometimes register your disapproval quietly and effectively. In the right circumstances, it is not a cop-out at all. You are not betraying your principles, and yet you are not really confronting in a way that will cause a scene. Moreover, sometimes when you *do* actively confront someone, they just dig their heels in further and defend themselves. Unless the offending person is really not paying attention, or is drunk or stoned, silence can make that person more uncomfortable than if you had challenged them and gotten their back up. I have found that, in some instances, silence can really be the loudest message.

HUMOR: A MINGLER'S GREATEST TOOL

Humor can be life-saving medicine in stressful social situations. Studies show that humor aids in relaxation, combats fear, decreases aggression, and helps people avoid fighting. Playful emotions are contagious, which is why they are often used to defuse social tension. For one thing, making a joke interrupts the conversational flow—in a good way—and reminds people of life outside the argument. This can ease tempers. It's like a snapping of a tension wire. When two people are having an argument, it is a serious and (at its best) logical back and forth; when you make a joke, you introduce the illogical, so it can be like a refreshing splash of water that breaks things up and stops the fight, at least temporarily. Whether it's silly or witty, humor can be a godsend.

However, it also can be a disaster, for when a joke goes bad it can make things worse. So be careful. When a humorous line works, often you will both laugh and you will be able to continue talking to each other about something else, or, if need be, it can allow you to easily part ways and each go find other conversational partners. The very best joke makes gentle fun of the fact that you were both getting too aggravated during the discussion.

Note: Most people do not have enough panache to successfully land a formal joke ("A Democrat, a Republican, and an Independent walked into a bar...") in a tense conversational moment. Don't try formal joke telling unless you are an expert. Humorous quips are your best bet.

Quick Quips to Have at Your Fingertips

The following lines, which are meant to be used when the conversation gets too hot, are just samples. You have to find what kind of humor works for your own style and personality. Most of the time, of course, your humorous remark will be tailor-made to fit the specific conversation.

Sample lines:

> "*Someday we'll look back on this, laugh nervously, and change the subject.*"

> "*Uh-oh. Is it time for your medication or mine?*"

> "*That wasn't me, that was my wounded inner child.*"

"You know how there are some days you should've stayed in bed? I'm having a whole year like that."

"Listen to us arguing! No wonder my mother always told me never to talk politics at a party. Why don't we talk about sex instead?"

"Do you feel like this conversation is having a nervous breakdown?"

"We'd better stop fighting. People will start to think we're married."

Of course, your tension-relieving line may fall flat. If you are brave enough to double down, you could always try one of these failed-joke recovery lines:

"Sorry. I think someone needs to take away my joking license."

"Oh well, that's what I get for trying to dispel an awkward moment with humor."

"I apologize. I was born without a funny bone and my prosthetic one seems to not be working well."

Self-Deprecating Humor

It's hard to say exactly why self-deprecation is funny. As E.B. White is famous for saying, "Analyzing humor is like dissecting a frog. The procedure kills the essence of both the frog and the funny—and then what's the point?" However, there's no question that this kind of humor can act as a conversational salve and is especially helpful at the office, when there is a lot of stress, a lot of competition, and usually a hierarchy. In the aforementioned study by Randstad USA, 72 percent of employees said that they feel stressed or anxious when heated political discussions or arguments occur in the workplace. Using self-deprecating humor puts people at ease—partly because it makes you vulnerable, gives over some of your power to the other person. And, according to researchers at Seattle University, it's especially effective to use self-deprecating humor if you are the boss.[8]

Picture this: You're in middle management and you and your department are working against a major deadline. It's late and everyone's nerves are frayed. You and one of your team members, while taking a break to have a bite to eat in the conference room, unwittingly fall into a discussion about a political issue. You're on different sides. Before you know it, the air is becoming thick with hostility. "Good god, look at me," you might say, "I don't even know what I'm talking about right now. I'm so fried you could put ketchup on me." Or, "Hey, don't mind me. Sometimes I forget I'm not guest-hosting 'Meet the Press.'"

How to Combat Sarcasm

Sarcasm is supposed to be funny, but it is usually just mean. Often it can feel like an attack. Next time somebody tosses a really sarcastic remark at you, try answering them ultra-literally. For example, if someone should say to you drippingly, "Oh, *right, good idea.* Let's feed the whole world, until we have no money left ourselves," you can answer very innocently with something like "Well I don't really think we can feed the whole world, but I'd like to try to feed some of it." Or if someone says, "Oh sure, why not? Let's not let *any* brown people into our country *ever again*," you can respond, "We should absolutely let any person, no matter what color or religion, immigrate legally or request asylum." The key is to respond very calmly as if you did not understand that they were being sarcastic.

Never fight sarcasm with sarcasm. That's just a recipe for argument escalation. Of course, this technique—responding literally—is still risky. If someone is pelting you with sarcastic barbs, you may have to get ready to change the conversation, or better yet, escape from the person altogether.

Let us make a special effort to stop communicating with each other, so we can have some conversation.

—Mark Twain

CHAPTER SIX

Diversionary Tactics

Sometimes your only viable option is to get out of the conversation—one way or another. Once the direction a conversation is taking has become untenable, your basic choices are to move to common ground, change the subject entirely, or leave that person altogether.

Some of you may ask, "Isn't it better to always leave immediately in these situations? Why even consider talking to someone once you have reached an ideological impasse that you can tell is about to lead to a fight?" There are several reasons that switching the topic instead of ditching the person is often either desirable or necessary. For one thing, you may be at a dinner party where you are physically stuck in one place; completely avoiding talking to the person would be inordinately rude. Or maybe you feel cornered for other reasons—the person is a business contact, a friend of a good friend, or a new neighbor. But a more important thing to keep in mind is this: In many cases when a conversation has veered into a tense area, that person or group could still be interesting or worthwhile to talk to. You don't want to get scared away from the whole interaction at the first sign of trouble simply because you've momentarily fallen into a dispute.

As we all know, distracting someone from the unpleasantness at hand is not a revolutionary idea. People have been avoiding conflict this way since the invention of the baby rattle. The main thing to remember here is that the fact that someone doesn't agree with you on a political issue does not have to be a conversation deal-breaker. You may be surprised. You may discover you both agree wholeheartedly on another, completely different issue. Or you may find that the very person you disagree with vehemently about the president happens to share your passion for (and your love of talking about) beer making, beekeeping, karate, or encaustic painting.

Many of the following methods for distracting, diverting, deterring, defusing, or de-intensifying will be familiar to you. And yes, in some instances the best thing for everyone involved is going to be for you to leave this person entirely and go find someone else to talk to. But before I provide you with your subject-switching tool kit and escape techniques, before I hand you the emergency rip cord for your impending conversational disaster, I just want to remind you that when things get heated, there still may be the possibility of finding common ground with that person.

SWIMMING TO AN ISLAND OF COMMON GROUND

The idea of finding common ground is something many people advocate as an admirable goal. But how exactly do you accomplish this goal when you are in the middle of an escalating argument where you are completely convinced you are right and feel your annoyance or anger overtaking your emotions? Who the hell feels like making concessions?

Common ground has become rather a loaded phrase. Some people interpret the term to mean a wishy-washy compromise, or a relinquishing of an important position. But keep in mind we are talking about socializing here, not policy making. Common ground in a social conversation is not like common ground in Congress. There are no far-reaching repercussions. Social conversation is a pastime in which the primary object is enjoyment and intellectual stimulation, or even career networking—not winning.

We've already learned how to test for "friend, foe, or fanatic." So let's say you've gone far enough in the conversation that you know this person is in fact squarely on the other side of an issue (foe), but they do not seem particularly unreasonable or combative. However, after you venture a little more into the subject at hand, you hit a big bump. Suddenly things are getting very strained. It seems you've arrived at a standoff. What do you do?

If you are feeling up to it, you should try to head for common ground. I like to think of it as "swimming" because it takes effort, you need to develop muscles to do it well, you have to travel a little distance, and it can be good for you. Also, when you are engaging in this process, it can often feel like you are paddling furiously and getting nowhere. First (as in swimming), do remember your breathing. Try to relax. Remind yourself that if what the person is espousing seems idiotic or wrong-headed to you, it's the *idea* that is "wrong," not the person.

One way to think of this tactic is to imagine taking a small step backward from the topic. Or even better, a step to one side. For instance, sometimes you disagree on the solution but can agree on the problem. You might disagree about whether or not our government should interfere with how content or algorithms are curated or regulated on social media sites like Facebook and Twitter, but you both agree that on these sites there is an alarming amount of disinformation, manipulation of elections, and hate mongering that is harmful to our democracy.

Where did the term "common ground" originate? One etymological theory that appeals to me is historical—that it comes from centuries ago, when people who were suspicious of each other would conduct their trading by placing their goods in an open clearing, in neutral territory. One group would hide, with their weapons at the ready, while the other group, also armed, would collect the goods, leaving behind their agreed-upon payment. It was a way for people who did not trust each other to make an exchange. I find this a helpful metaphor. When you find common ground in conversation, you are both agreeing—if warily so—not to attack each other while interacting.

Swimming to an island of common ground is not exactly a diversionary tactic; it's more positive than a simple diversion. To find common ground can be tricky, but rewarding. If conversation is a verbal dance, finding common ground should be a do-si-do away from the political argument you're having or are about to have.

Sidestepping It

One evening not too long ago, I was invited to a sit-down dinner in Brooklyn. Most of the other guests were people I did not know. The man beside me at the table was the host's brother-in-law, an economics professor visiting from Drake University in Iowa. Our conversation turned naturally to the severe weather that had been occurring in that state; the reports of extremely bad flooding had been all over the news. Soon we were discussing the devastation caused in other parts of the country by recent hurricanes, tornados, and wildfires. "I do think we are experiencing extreme weather," the professor said, "and that global warming is happening, but it's definitely not being caused by anything we are doing as humans."

I responded that everything I had read in a dozen respected journals and magazines refuted this claim, and that we were going to be in major trouble within fifty years if we didn't do something to counteract it. He answered that he was highly suspicious of that data, that the evidence was politically motivated. From the pedantic way he was talking I could tell there was going to be no upside to arguing about it with him. And he probably was thinking the same thing about me. We were not going to find common ground on climate change; I needed to change the topic.

I decided it was time to trot out one of my customary lighten-the-mood quips. I laughed and said, "Well I guess the aliens need to hurry up and come down and save us."

He laughed also and then said, "Too bad aliens don't exist."

"What do you mean?" I asked him.

"I mean there is no life on any other planets. At least not intelligent life."

I set my wine glass down and turned to him. "Wait. I was kidding about aliens coming to save us. But obviously there has to be life on other planets *somewhere* out there. How can there not be? Just look up at the sky at night. There are 10 billion stars in our galaxy *alone*. And there are billions and billions of galaxies in the universe. They say there are as many stars as there are grains of sand on Earth."

"Sorry to disappoint you," smiled the professor, "but there's actually been a recent Oxford study proving that there is slim to no chance of other intelligent life anywhere in the known universe."

"In all of space? But, but..." I sputtered, "it's just human-centric hubris to think we are somehow the only ones. In the whole universe? That makes no sense to me. I don't know about this recent study, but to me it's like when people used to believe the sun revolved around the earth. That was only a few centuries ago. With all our technology, we are still just scientific babies in this area." He just smiled knowingly again and, nodding, said he could understand why a lot of people did not want to accept the truth: that we are alone in the universe.

Now, I'd like to be able to tell you that the professor was the one getting overwrought, but sadly, I have to confess it was me. I admit that I get overly excited when it comes to this subject—to me it is so obvious! Not that there are definitely alien civilizations that look like ours, or that we will ever meet any extraterrestrials, but that it is likely that some intelligent life forms exist *somewhere*. It seems to me the theories that they *don't* exist are based entirely on our own human presumptions about what any advanced civilization's relationship to space exploration would be (that is, that if they were out there, they would already be visiting us). And yet, of course, I have no actual proof. It's quite possible I have simply watched too much *Star Trek*.

After a few more minutes of impassioned protests to the professor, I realized this felt a little like arguing about religion. I decided in the case of this topic, unlike with the topic of climate change, I could "sidestep" into some common ground within the topic.

I turned to him and said, "Well, one thing I'll concede: I certainly can agree that all these crazy stories of alien abductions you hear about are not real. And that photos people have taken of UFOs are fake, or otherwise explainable." (PS, I actually have an open mind about some of the photos. But I wasn't going to say that. *Shhhh*.)

We both clinked our wine glasses, having finally arrived at our "island," and conversed about some of the more outlandish claims among the alien abductee stories. I then conceded that I certainly had no evidence of the existence of aliens, I just was going to keep hoping, and we went on to talking about our favorite sci-fi movies. The rest of the evening was interesting and upbeat.

Some topics are better common ground candidates than others. Admittedly, it's much harder to swim to common ground when you are talking about the bigger, more incendiary issues of the day like global warming. And of course, there may be some subjects about which you don't feel you can (or should) reach common ground, even if you wanted to try. At least not in twenty minutes at a party. But when you can reach some kind of common ground without being untrue to your beliefs, it can be good for your social well-being.

Misery Loves Company, or Finding a Common "Enemy"

In general, I think it's best to be as positive as possible when mingling. People who are positive make others feel good, and that tends to enhance the flow of conversation. On the other hand, when two people share displeasure or fear or pain at the same thing or person, it can be a bonding experience. Also, it's an unalterable fact that much of human beings' humorous repartee involves complaining. So, next time you run into a person who feels the opposite way you do about Trump, before you blow a gasket, try to find someone you BOTH can hate: a local politician, a celebrity in the news, or an objectionable legislation that has just been passed that you both agree is terrible—new parking rules, new local zoning laws, the new mega shopping mall down the street. Does the garbage pickup or construction going on in the neighborhood keep you both awake? Does the TSA practice of making you take your shoes off in the airport make you crazy?

There are a few simple rules to follow when indulging in this kind of negative common ground:

1. Be sure the other person also wants to complain about what you think is horrible. You'll be able to tell whether or not they are "with you" after about ten seconds of broaching the topic.

2. Always try to use humor and warmth when complaining. You have to make the other person understand that you may be sharing how you feel, but you are in no way bringing a bad vibe with you into the party. That is, you are happy to meet someone who feels the way you do on this subject, but you are not going to be negative about everything.

3. Don't let your commiserating subject lead you into an argument. The only danger with this technique is that sometimes if you complain about the fact that local taxes are going up, or that you hate the new highway that's being built through the nearby woodland, it can lead to political subjects on which you diverge.

Of course, you can't just start talking about random things you hate. Your "common enemy" topic should stem from problematic conversation you are having.

Here is an example:

Two people are at a business cocktail party. The conversation has led to the subject of the vaccination controversy. Person A takes an anti-vaccination stance, saying that the new measles outbreak has nothing to do with people refusing to get their kids inoculated, that vaccines contain harmful substances that can make you feel sick or can cause serious health problems later, and that the government (or Big Pharma) has no business telling people what medical care to receive. The other person, Person B, believes inoculations are essential to the nation's health and very rarely make anyone sick, and they can't understand why anyone would want to go back to the days before we had protection against these dangerous diseases. It's become apparent that this is a completely polarized discussion.

Person A: I'm against requisite vaccinations. I think it should be up to parents.

Person B: Well, I'm *for* them. It's not fair to put everyone's health at risk.

(Awkward pause in the conversation.)

Person A: *(searching for a common "enemy")* Well, sometimes it doesn't even matter about vaccinations. Have you heard about that new fungus that's been appearing in New York and New Jersey called *Candida auris?* Apparently there's no treatment for this disease.

Person B: Yes, it's horrible and scary.

Person A: I agree. Very scary. Where else in the world have they found it occurring—do you know?

While it's not a very cheery discussion, A and B have managed to move out of feuding territory—at least for the time being.

(In this case, the common enemy is an actual disease, not merely a poisonous politician!)

Shared Interests

Sometimes in order to get to any kind of common ground you may have to abandon the specific topic altogether, then perhaps return to it later. You might discover another political issue you can agree on, or at least debate rationally. But often we need to backtrack all the way out of politics and find lifestyle elements we have in common. Are you both in the same professional field? Do you both have babies? Do you both have allergies? Are you both allergic to babies? Perhaps you are both in a book club, a bowling league, or a monthly card game. You might share a love of dogs, or a love of a particular vacation spot or of a TV show. Shared love of TV shows can be good if you like the same one. But be careful. As I said in chapter two, it can also be a divider.

Once you have connected via this kind of common ground, then the other subjects will be easier to deal with. The more agreeable the conversation you have, the more you begin to appreciate the other person as a person; and then when they say something that might otherwise provoke you, you will have a common language, in a sense, on which to build. Remember, connection is king.

In order to get away from the dangerous conversation and reach the shores of the shared interest, however, you are going to need to know how to change the subject smoothly and easily.

DEFLECTION: SIX SUBJECT-CHANGING TECHNIQUES

More often than not, when you are mingling with the enemy, things are apt to get too dicey to find any kind of common ground. The most obvious thing to do is to change the subject altogether.

But sometimes that's easier said than done. Frequently the other person is worked up and is therefore talking loudly and quickly, which can make changing course difficult. Here are some handy subject-changing tricks.

Bridge Building

When executing this technique, you need to figure out exactly where you want to go in the conversation, and then find a connector or a linking subject to get you there. What you need to do is imagine all the possible connections between the two subjects, select one, and then head for that "bridge." A good way to think about the process is to imagine you and your conversational partner are currently on one side of the river; you want to get both of you to the other side. The key is to find some material with which to build a bridge to carry you to where you want to be.

I interviewed a woman, Patricia, who recounted the following tale of a tricky social situation where she used this technique. She was at a large celebratory party for one of her husband's important business contacts. She ended up seated at dinner next to the host's sister (so Patricia needed to really be on her best behavior). It was in late October, right before the 2016 presidential election, and politics was an inevitable topic. Patricia was a Democrat and a Hillary supporter, and had a lot of trepidation about a Trump presidency. During dinner, the sister began pontificating about how the Democratic Party and the Republican Party were exactly alike in every way—both corrupt and horrible—and the only conscionable thing a person could do was to vote for Jill Stein, the Green Party candidate. She was adamant that this was really the only choice for any progressive-minded person.

Now this was pushing Patricia's buttons for many reasons—not the least of which was the fear that in a close race, any liberal "third party" candidate would throw the race to the conservatives in key states. She could feel her ire rising, but knew, for her husband's sake, that she could not afford to lose her temper with her dinner companion, who was quite obviously not open to any other opinion but the one she was spouting. Patricia decided she needed to move the conversation elsewhere—fast. What she really had been hoping to talk to the sister about was the town where this party was being held, because she and her husband were thinking of moving there.

"It would certainly be interesting to have two physicians in the White House," Patricia said carefully, remembering that not only Stein but also her husband was a doctor.

"Well, that's not exactly the point, but why?"

"I just think doctors have a particular way of analyzing, of working through a problem. They are solution oriented," said Patricia.

"Right, well, Stein's policies are the thing that will begin to turn things around."

"Yes, I hear what you are saying. Stein has some good ideas. But by the way, speaking of doctors, I hope you don't mind my asking, but are there good doctors in this area? My husband and I are thinking about moving here. And are the schools good?"

Bridge building requires shifting your focus a bit during conversation, so that as you listen to the other person speak, you concentrate not only on your response to the person's comment or question, but also on where you want the conversation to go next. I don't mean that you should not pay attention to the present conversation. The best minglers always at least give the *impression* that they are fascinated by whatever is being said to them. As much as possible, the conversation must appear to flow naturally, as if it is taking its own course. But if you are on your toes, you can make a swift transition to a subject of your choosing before the other person knows what hit them.

Admittedly, some subjects are harder to move away from than others. And there are some people who are adamantly determined to talk about whatever it is they are determined to talk about. If you really get good at changing subjects, however, you can pull the switcheroo on anyone.

Free Association

Another way to change subjects is to use free association. This technique works best when you are in a group rather than one-on-one; it is more playful and creative and therefore more easily received if more than two people are involved in the conversation. For example, in the above Jill Stein scenario, if Patricia had been standing in a group as the sister was extolling the virtues of the Green Party, she could have taken the word "green" and let it lead her to another word, the first word that popped into her mind. For instance, she could have thought, *green—tea*. Then she might have remarked in a playful manner that she wondered whether more people in the Green Party drink green tea than coffee. Having landed on the subject of coffee, she could have then quickly added that she herself was trying to give up drinking so much coffee, or that she just recently had the best cup of coffee in the world, or did anyone know where the best place in the neighborhood was for a cup of coffee? If that seemed too frivolous and lightweight as a transition and she wanted to stay on a more serious topic, she could have led the group to a discussion of how some studies have shown that America's coffee habit is harming the environment (as they are now finding caffeine has traveled from sewer systems all the way to rural streams).

Free association is more flexible and openended than bridge building. That is, you aren't necessarily trying to get from point A to point B; you are simply moving away from point A. One reason free association can work well is that the subject you move to is also often right on the tip of everyone else's brain. The change should usually seem perfectly natural and not at all forced.

Pole Vaulting

This tactic takes a bit more courage than most. It can be a little tough to do. But if you can pole vault well, you can actually leap right over to your desired topic. Let's say you are in a conversation with someone who is adamantly against the legalization of marijuana and is getting worked up into a lather about it. "The use of marijuana leads directly to opiate deaths, which are ravaging this country!" they are saying to you in a raised voice. Now, you don't happen to believe this; you believe the recreational use of marijuana should be legal and regulated like alcohol. But you don't want to argue. If you want to perform a classic pole vault, you say, "Not too sure about that. But hey, buddy, we haven't talked about the game today! Could you believe those Knicks? They were amazing!" Whooooosh! You leap right over to a completely different topic.

This is not a subtle maneuver, and some observers may judge you as having the attention span of a gnat. But so what? It can be a quick solution to a bad moment. The trick is to keep moving forward with your new topic, to cement it as the new area of conversation. Don't allow the other person to drag you back to the original topic.

Warning: There are some conversations where this technique is not applicable. Do not attempt to pole vault to another topic if someone is having a serious conversation about a mass killing or the cure for cancer. You will be seen as incredibly callous.

Here are some typical pole-vaulting lines:

"Well I don't know about that, but there's one thing I do know about: I'm hungry! Will someone pass the turkey? How did Ben make this gravy? It's delicious."

"Hey, not to change the subject, but I saw this awesome thing on the news today..."

"Interesting. I'll have to look that up. But wait, I wanted to ask you before I forget..."

Sense and Insensibility

A technique favored by many a shy or passive person, here you simply pretend you didn't hear the remark at all. It is the most passive subject-switching method there is. You simply become oblivious.

Here's how you do it: Keep a slight smile on your face as a person is saying the thing you find off-putting. Do not respond; never even incline your head to show that what they said has registered. The trick to the "sense and insensibility" ploy is you've got to become an emotionless rock and let the offensive or inflammatory remark flow over you like rain. It's somewhat different from the previously described "power of silence" stance, because with sense and insensibility, you want the person to believe that you simply did not hear them (as opposed to being too appalled to answer them). As with the pole vault above, you must immediately start talking about something else entirely.

Pleading Ignorance

This can be especially useful when you are faced with a "man (or woman)-splainer," a blowhard, or an otherwise overbearing person. You know the type: someone who is not listening at all but who is spewing phrases like "I've done more research on this than anyone I know," or "You'd have to be a complete idiot not to know that..." With this technique, you have to be willing to swallow your pride. But there's probably no way to have a rational discussion with this person anyway, and pleading ignorance can really deflate the blowhard—like putting a pin into a hot air balloon.

Try countering with, "Hmm. I don't really know anything about that." Or if that's too ego wounding, go with, "That doesn't sound quite right, but I confess I don't really know enough to discuss it. Let's talk about something else." Or the classic version: "I have to take the fifth on this subject, for fear that my answer may incriminate me—in your eyes." (Smile.)

There are times when, especially when you are with a know-it-all, the best thing you can do is to become a know-nothing.

Toasting

There are many ways you can use toasting in mingling. Toasting is an old-fashioned custom that is underutilized today. As a subject-changing device, toasting can be both a conversation punctuation point and a mood elevator. For instance: "Well, let us drink to a difference of opinion, to good company, and most of all to our host!" "Okay, but in any case, here's to the best roast beef in culinary history!" Or, "We should get back to that subject later. Right now I want to make a toast to the beginning of spring!" You can toast to almost anything. But *do* be sure to have a glass in your hand.

THE EJECTOR SEAT: ESSENTIAL ESCAPE MANEUVERS

Let's face it. While I have been encouraging you throughout this chapter to reach common ground, change the subject, and otherwise not give up on the person, many times you will just want out—all the way out. When you feel as though you are in danger of insulting the other person for being an idiot, or blaming them for being the devil—or that the other person is about to accuse you of the same—the only thing to do is to get away from the person altogether.

Please note that these maneuvers cannot be executed if you are at a sit-down dinner. If you are seated at a table, usually the best you can do is wait for a pause in the conversation, then turn to talk to the person on the other side of you.

The Buffet Bye-Bye: Easy Exit Lines

The most common escape strategy is to politely excuse yourself for a real or a feigned necessity. Most of us are very familiar with this simple exit maneuver, but here are some standard exit lines:

"I'd like to get into this subject further, but first I need another drink. Will you excuse me?"

"I don't know about that, but there's one thing I do know about: I'm hungry! I must get something to eat."

"*Well, that certainly is a very interesting idea, but I feel the call of nature* [have to visit the sandbox/have to pee/need to find the restroom]."

Note: It's quite possible the person will want to follow you to wherever it is you say you are going. For that reason, the best line to use is what I call the "telephone line," or the "cell-out": "This is all quite fascinating, but I promised my babysitter/husband/boss/daughter/contractor that I would check in with them and I think they've been texting me." Because it would be rude to use your phone while you are in the middle of a conversation, this gives you a good excuse to leave the company of the person in question. The "cell-out" is also perfect for when you are standing in line, or on a train or an airplane, and you do not feel like continuing the conversation. Let's face it: checking your phone is everyone's default instinct anyway. You simply go back to being engrossed in your phone the way you would normally be.

The Human Sacrifice

One man I interviewed recounted an uncomfortable exchange he got into at his wife's high school reunion. He knew hardly anyone there, so he was mingling over by the food table. (The food area is the best place for talking to strangers as you have a purpose for being there, and if all else fails, you can concentrate on eating.) He struck up a conversation with a woman named Deena over how good the shrimp were. One thing led to another, and before long they were talking energetically about their careers and their families. He found Deena interesting, outspoken, and funny. Eventually the conversation turned to politics.

"It's so amazing to me how racist our country is now," she said. "Every single person who voted for Trump is a racist, whether they know it or not."

The man, himself a conservative, had not voted for Trump, but he told me he had a few friends who had, and who he was sure were misguided but not racists. One of them, in fact, was African American.

"I don't think you can really say that," the man ventured.

"It's *completely true!* You can't not know that!" said Deena, looking irritated. Her whole demeanor had changed. She looked as though she was ready for a fight.

At that moment, as luck would have it, out of the corner of his eye, the man spotted a woman he had met earlier, heading toward them (well, toward the food, anyway). And as further luck would have it, he actually remembered her name.

"Suzanne," he called to the woman, holding out his arm to her in a welcoming manner, "have you met Deena?" Suzanne approached them, and as Deena was shaking hands with her, the man uttered a quick, "Excuse me" and—blessedly—was out.

This is the ever-useful "human sacrifice," where you find someone else to take over with the person you would like to get away from. It's a bit like finding someone else to dance with your partner rather than just leaving them alone on the dance floor. It is a time-honored method for escaping from someone at a party, though most people don't know it by this name, and most are too ashamed to admit they practice this technique. However, I see it done all the time, at almost every type of social function. It's a clever gambit because it poses as a social grace—that is, that you are introducing two people who don't know each other. However, when mingling with the enemy, you will want to, if at all possible, try to make sure that the new person (the "sacrifice") is on the same political side as the person you are escaping from. This is the kindest version of the human sacrifice. In fact, if you can manage this, it's not a human sacrifice at all, but a meritorious match-making maneuver.

Counterfeit Search

As old as the hills, this is just a version of the time-honored "I think I hear my mother calling" excuse. If things are reaching a boiling point in your conversation, just place your hand gently on the forearm of the person, in order to interrupt the flow of their tirade, and say, "I'm so sorry, I *do* want to hear more about this, but there is someone here I promised my boss I would talk to. I need to get to them before they leave." Or "Hold that thought. My wife is signaling me and I have to see what she wants."

Shake and Break

I don't know if this extraordinary story is true, but a friend of mine swears it is. My friend's friend, who I'll call Sofia, was on vacation in Florida and had gone to a bar with some girlfriends to soak up the local nightlife. She got into a conversation with a man who was flirting with her. Supposedly, at a certain point the man revealed to Sofia that he was a member of the Flat Earth Society—for real. He believes that the "round earthers" (people who believe the earth is a sphere) were perpetrating a grand conspiracy, that all the photos of the earth taken from space, or from high mountains, were fake. He believes the earth is flat, with the North Pole in the middle, and a wall of ice around the edges, which is Antarctica. (According to a YouGov poll, two percent of the US population believe the world is flat.[9] That's about six and a half million people.)

Apparently this "flat earther" started trying to recruit Sofia, or at least convince her of the validity of his theory. I don't know how she finally threw the nutty guy off, but in an extreme case like this, I have found the best course of action is to use the "shake and break." This exit leaves no room for interpretation. You are saying goodbye in no uncertain terms.

As you are smiling at the person or otherwise responding facially to what they are saying, stick your hand out until they instinctively take hold of it, or just grab their hand. Shake it until they either stop speaking or at least slow down. Smile warmly and tell them, "It's been interesting talking with you." Then turn quickly and walk swiftly away, leaving them (ahem)—flat.

THE PARTY PAUSE

Once in a while you may find yourself thrown off balance. Perhaps you were not prepared for the heated political discussion you have witnessed between two friends and it has unnerved you. Or you need to recover from losing your own cool with someone. Don't you wish sometimes that you were a magician, or a witch, and you could snap your fingers and everything would just stop for a second, so you could regain your composure? The party pause is just that. It's a time-out you take for yourself.

If there is any outside space at your social gathering, step outside—to look at the garden, walk around the yard, look at the stars. Otherwise, go to the bedroom where all the coats are, and pretend to be checking your phone for important messages. Go into another room and look at the books on the bookshelf. Take deep breaths for five or ten minutes, then go back to the party and have a good time—talking to someone new.

GRACEFUL RETREAT

No matter how valiant your efforts, there are instances when you will feel the need to bail on the social event altogether. This won't happen very often. Most parties you attend will be civilized enough that no matter what conversations you find yourself in, you won't actually be compelled to leave. But there are going to be those (hopefully very rare) times when, for your sanity, the physical safety of others, and your spiritual well-being, you are going to need to leave the gathering altogether.

Whatever you do, don't leave in a huff. Don't make a scene. If possible, concoct a believable excuse for why you are leaving early (your kid is sick, you have a migraine, you forgot about an early meeting the next day). For your own peace of mind, as you are leaving, visualize emerging from an ocean with big scary waves, or coming inside to escape a bad rainstorm. While you are looking forward to getting psychologically warmed up and cozy, it's no use remaining stressed about or angry at the ocean or the storm, right?

Be sure to say goodbye to whoever is hosting the party before you leave, even if what you see as their idiotic ideas about tax reform or immigration policies have riled you. Just shake it off, and live to (not) fight another day.

Our prime purpose in this life is to help others. And if you can't help them, at least don't hurt them.

—Dalai Lama

CHAPTER SEVEN

Helping Others: Being a Social Diplomat

The real heroes and heroines of today's social universe are not the people who give the most luxurious parties, the people you read about on page six, or the people who can chat up anyone, anytime, but instead are the people who step in unselfishly to save the day when they see conversational trouble brewing nearby. I call these people social diplomats.

It's hard enough to deal with getting out of a political argument when you're in the middle of it, but to volunteer to break up someone else's argument as an act of kindness to the group goes above and beyond the call of duty. Social diplomats are folks who, instead of just watching as the conversation turns into a combat zone, dash headlong into the fray for the sake of the harmony of the party at large. There are not very many people who are willing to do this, though I believe more people should be. Whether you are (1) in a conversation with two people who are headed for a brouhaha, (2) simply an alert "bystander" who spots trouble from across the room, or (3) hosting the party and therefore see it as your responsibility, helping to keep the peace is a noble pursuit. If more of us were willing to do it, we'd all have a lot less party anxiety—and a lot less shouting in general.

PEACEKEEPING MISSIONS

To mediate or not to mediate, that is the question. Whether 'tis nobler in the mind to interfere or to just let people sling their arrows where they will—even when you can see those arrows are headed nowhere good. It's not always easy to tell whether you should try to step into someone else's conversation or leave it alone. Sometimes the people in question are friends whose personalities and tendencies you know well enough to be able to foresee trouble. Other times you may just get a spidey sense that there is something dangerous percolating nearby. A general rule to follow is this: If you are not convinced it's leading to overt animosity—in other words, to a hostile argument instead of a lively discussion—and therefore constitutes a potential detriment to everyone's enjoyment of the occasion, do nothing. Otherwise, here are some "social savior" techniques to try.

The White Flag

Picture this. You are surveying the party and just happen to notice a group of people across the room, where one man is gesticulating wildly and another man is shaking his head repeatedly and shuffling his feet. You know they are really going at it; you can tell by the negatively charged energy coming from them. It looks as though all they need is a spark to explode.

Here you come to save the day! Go ahead, don your invisible cape and get over there. But remember, you don't want to actually fly in dramatically like Superman. You have to sort of sidle in when you have an opportunity—to enter their sphere innocently as if you are not aware there is anything untoward afoot. The main thing to remember when you get there is that you simply need to break the spell, to interrupt the current interaction. In most cases you won't have to be brilliant or do anything too drastic. Usually people simply need a little push to get them going in a different direction, someone to wave a white flag in front of them to remind them where they are.

It's usually advisable not to take sides or indicate in any way that one of them is more at fault than another (even if you do in fact side with one of them on the particular issue at hand). Unless, of course, one person is obviously the aggressor and the other person is cowering against the wall, whimpering, "But I didn't even *see* the news today, I swear..." In that unlikely case, you can rescue the victim by pulling them out of harm's way, with a "Sorry to interrupt this interrogation, but I need Charlie over here for a sec."

We all want to encourage other people to be their best selves. I think of this kind of altruistic maneuver as waving the white flag of peace. Here are some sample white flag lines:

"What are you two doing? Remember, a cocktail party divided against itself cannot stand!"

"Hey you guys, if you can't say something nice, say it in French."

"You know, I can lend you some boxing gloves if you'd both like to step outside."

"Listen, studies show that Americans are worried about politically motivated violence. But let's not have any at this particular gathering, okay?"

Note: As with the breaking up of a physical fight, it may take more than one try to break the spell of the conflict. Sometimes you will have to use more than one of these lines, if the first one proves ineffectual.

Tell an "Ouch" Joke

Never underestimate the power of silliness. This kind of joke telling can take the heat out of a discussion—it can slow it down or lessen the tension. It's like letting the air out of the tires. However, because these are dumb jokes, it's a bit like falling on your sword. People are not going to exactly see you as erudite after you spout one of these beauties. But it's the essential corniness of the joke that acts as the bucket of cold water you are throwing on them. If you get groans, so much the better.

Just to be clear, there are a lot of political jokes or witticisms you could tell that are *not* corny, such as "The consensus after the election is that 100% of Americans think 50% of Americans have lost their minds." But these more subtle jokes might just fuel the fire you are trying to put out. Your joke for this technique needs to be one that could inspire the proverbial drumbeat that comes after a bad joke. (Ta-DA...da.)

I myself can never remember jokes, but if you are someone who can, here are a couple of good "bad" ones to use:

"Always remember: when arguing, you should never throw dirt on your opponent. All you do is lose ground."

"You guys arguing? Hey: Do you know what debate is for?"
(What?)
"It's for catching da fish."

(For times when you hear someone arguing about "America" or "being an American")

"If you are American when you go into the bathroom, and American when you come out, what are you in the bathroom?
(What?)
"European."

"Did you hear this one? Three conspiracy theorists walk into a bar. You can't tell me that's just a coincidence!"

"What would you call the USA if everyone lived in their cars?"
(What?)
"An incarnation."

Culture Shocking

One evening during the holiday season, a time when tension is usually at its highest (health clinics should offer not just flu shots but bad mood shots), I was at a large potluck dinner and noticed two guests arguing. I did not hear the actual argument—I could only catch a word here and there—but one of them shouted, "*Something something* LIBERAL MEDIA!" and I heard the other shout back, "*Something something something* FOX NEWS!"

Taking my life in my hands, I went over to them, touched them both on their arms and said sternly, "No soup for you!" And then I smiled and sort of squeezed their arms in a friendly way. As if to say, "Hey get a grip, you two." This kind of thing doesn't always work, but this time it did. I was lucky that both of them got the *Seinfeld* reference and laughed sheepishly.

Depending on the situation—where you are, what the occasion is, what generation everyone there is—this device can be highly effective. It depends on people getting your references, of course, so you do have to know your audience somewhat, either by temperament or generation. But even if they don't get the reference, you still may have derailed them, even while embarrassing yourself a little. (Remember, it's an honorable sacrifice.)

These lines work like tiny verbal Tasers jolting the person away from the current path they are on. It breaks their concentration. It's similar to what you do with children when you clap and say, "Hey! Stop that!" Ideally you should get a laugh, and then everyone should be able to take a beat and go back to being civilized. In spite of the above *Seinfeld* example, "culture shocking" works best when you are actually present for the developing conflict, so that you can hear the whole conversation and choose a line that is appropriate.

Examples:

"No soup for you!" (*Seinfeld*)

"Fasten your seatbelts, it's going to be a bumpy night!" (*All About Eve*)

"Forget it Jake, it's Chinatown." (*Chinatown*)

"Danger, Will Robinson!" (*Lost in Space*)

"Just when I thought I was out, they pull me back in." (*The Godfather Part III*)

"What we've got here is a failure to communicate." (*Cool Hand Luke*)

"Houston, we have a problem." (*Apollo 13*)

"Let's make it work, people!" (*Project Runway*)

"You know nothing, Jon Snow." (*Game of Thrones*)

"That's what she said." (*The Office*)

"That's, just, like, your opinion, man." (*The Big Lebowski*)

"Lions and tigers and bears, oh my!" (*The Wizard of Oz*)

Arbitration

Sometimes, for one reason or another, you may feel it's worth the effort to try to mediate, to facilitate the discussion at the same time you help them bring it down a notch. For example, let's say you are at a social event and are walking by two guys you know. We'll call them Dan and Stan. You hear them arguing bitterly about the issue of assisted suicide.

"Euthanasia is compassionate medical treatment for people with painful terminal illnesses," Dan is saying forcefully. "It's not fair to make them suffer."

Stan, obviously upset, responds, "It's just wrong. It's murder. And who decides when it should happen? Where is the line drawn? Who is sick enough? What if they can get better but they are too much in despair to know?"

"But it's up to the PERSON," says Dan, his voice rising. "How can someone else force them to live in pain?! Who are you to decide *that* for them?"

"Excuse me," you say, joining them, "I think both of you have a point." (You are now operating as the arbitrator.) "It's really a complicated issue."

"It's not complicated; this guy doesn't believe in the sanctity of life," Stan complains.

"I don't think that's exactly what he means," you say. "We've all had experiences of knowing someone or watching someone who is dying an excruciating death. I think Dan's just saying he thinks they should have some rights."

"But..." Stan protests.

"On the other hand," you add quickly, turning to Dan, "Stan has a really good point. If we legalize euthanasia, how do we ever regulate it? Who is going to decide who lives and who dies? I know this is one I puzzle over a lot."

Hopefully by now the two have calmed down enough that you can all three continue the debate in a civilized manner. The key to being a "mingling arbitrator" is that, while you can agree with one person more than another, you have to help the two people listen to each other and appreciate each other's point of view.

How well this technique works depends a lot on the argument, the participants, and your arbitration skills. The main thing you have to remember is to stay really even tempered when you speak, no matter what the emotional level of the disputees is. You don't want to call attention to their hotheadedness. You are going to simply bring the conversation back to normal with your own behavior.

THE FINE ART OF DISTRACTION

The art of distraction is similar to the subject-changing techniques in chapter six except that you are changing the subject of other people's conversations rather than a conversation you are in. The following ploys are to be used when you see trouble from afar—instances where you have not been part of the conversation. You are going to have to approach and interrupt the people who are showing signs of losing it. When this is successful, the arguers should immediately be redirected to a totally different tack.

Game Playing

Game playing, or poll taking, has always been one of my favorite mingling techniques. It's fun at the same time that it accomplishes a purpose. In this case, the purpose is to distract people from arguing. It's upbeat and reminds people of the true spirit of mingling. What you do is become, for a minute or two, a little bit like a camp counselor. The trick is to act as though you are bringing people into a game that has been ongoing in the rest of the party. This disrupts the flow of conversation and, at the same time, reminds the arguers that they are part of a larger group even though they are having a very intense one-on-one discussion. Below are some sample "games." However, if you're a creative person, you can probably invent your own that work just as well, or better.

> *"Do you mind if I interrupt? I need to ask you guys a question. Did you see the latest episode of* [name of TV show], *and what did you think of it?"*

"Hi. I'm taking a poll. If you were on a deserted island and could have only one kind of food, would you rather it be pizza, chocolate, or smoked salmon?"

"Both of you shut your eyes, right now. Okay, now tell me what color shirt the other person is wearing."

"Hi. I'm taking a time travel survey. Would you rather travel 100 years back in history or 100 years into the future?"

"Hello! This group seems like it needs to relax. Which would you prefer, if you could beam yourselves there right now: a hot tub or hot springs?"

Put Some English on It

This one definitely isn't for everyone. It has to suit your style. What you are going to do is interject obscure vocabulary in order to stun people out of their anger. Employing fancy verbal footwork will often give people pause.

I've never actually tried this myself, but I interviewed a man who uses this ploy sometimes. He is obviously a word master; I think it might be from doing crossword puzzles all his life. Anyway, he has a thing for abstruse English. One evening this man was at a school fundraiser and happened to be standing in the vicinity of a serious argument that had arisen about a #MeToo story that had just erupted on social media that day. This was a story where there was a vehement online debate about the validity of the accusations. A woman and man were raising their voices and it was getting ugly, and going nowhere.

He turned to the angry couple. "Well! Neither one of you has *alexithymia*, that's for sure," he said with a gentle smile.

(Alexithymia is an inability to identify and express or describe one's feelings.)

They stared at him for a second, discombobulated. The woman said, "What?" Then the man who had been arguing with her excused himself and walked away. Now, while this was not exactly the Treaty of Paris, the unexpected comment did break up the fight.

Here are some other examples:

"I sense one of you may be tergiversating." (being evasive)

"Which one of you is guilty of fomentation?" (the stirring up of violent sentiment)

"STOP already. Just listening to you is aggravating my allodoxaphobia." (fear of opinions)

"What quodlibet *are we discussing over here?"* (a topic for philosophical or theological discussion)

"Neither one of you is suasible." (susceptible to persuasion)

Please keep in mind: You are not using these words to seem smart or impress anyone. It's only that this kind of thing can derail a conversation. At the very least people will stop what they are talking about to ask you what you mean. Of course, they may think you are a weirdo. But either way you will have just robbed them of their argumentative energy for the time being.

When All Else Fails: Sing

This may sound insane, but there are experts who will tell you that when people are really fighting, sometimes what works to break it up is to start singing. I know, I know, most people would never want to do this. But if it's a really ugly altercation and you happen to be an extrovert who is also a frustrated performer, now may be the time. I recommend something like "Don't Worry, Be Happy," "Put on a Happy Face," or "Que Sera, Sera." Or, if you are really adventurous, Lady Gaga's "Bad Romance."

Warning: Employ this technique at your own risk. It could work like a charm, or you could get a punch in the nose.

BEWARE OF DEATH BY TRIANGULATION

One of the dangers you face when you are infiltrating a discussion for the purpose of peacemaking is triangulation. Triangulation is a manipulation whereby one person who is having an issue with someone else uses a third party to validate their feelings or support their point of view. This is more commonly known as getting sucked into a fight.

Your risk of being triangulated may increase when you enter a conversation in progress with a couple (meaning two people in any kind of long-term relationship). This happens to me sometimes when I stay overnight with good friends of mine who are married. One is a lifelong Democrat and the other a staunch Republican, and they tend to bicker a lot about politics, at least when other people are around. Whether they are talking about organic farming or the voting rights of ex-convicts—or whatever happens to be in the news that day—they are always looking for another person to help them process their conflicts. "Hey Jeanne," one will say, while we are all three making dinner and I am focusing on chopping something (and am therefore caught off guard), "Did you read about the bill the Senate passed yesterday? Don't you agree that it's the worst move ever? Please help me enlighten my darling spouse."

Not surprisingly, when it comes to couples, any dispute is usually about much more than politics; the friction often bleeds into, or extends from, their marital issues, which is why you want to stay as neutral as possible. It's dangerous territory.

Be on the lookout for triangulation, even when it is not perpetrated by spouses but just by two or more random people embroiled in an argument. It can be awkward at best and horrible at worst. Stay alert for the kinds of comments listed below, which will more than likely be addressed to you immediately upon your joining the conversation:

"Oh good, here you are. We've been trying to settle an argument."

"Wait: let's get another opinion on this from someone sensible."

"This lovely idiot thinks our country is doing just fine. Can you believe that?"

"Okay, pretend you don't know either of us. What do you think of _____?"

Hear the warning bells going off? You should. You've just stepped on a landmine, or are about to. You are being asked to take sides in no uncertain terms. At the first indication you have entered a booby-trapped area like this, it's best to retreat from the conversation as gingerly as you can. Either physically escape ("Oh wait, I forgot my drink, I left it over by the piano") or conversationally escape (by changing the subject using one of the techniques in chapter six). You can always stay and try to mediate, if you feel you can. Or say, "Hey you guys, please don't drag me into this."

Of course, a line like the ones listed above does not necessarily mean trouble. Sometimes it is just an entrée to an interesting discussion. And if the conversation is rational, respectful, and stimulating, you should certainly feel free to go ahead and take sides. Always remember: all of the evasive techniques in this book are to be used to avoid having a fight, not to avoid thought-provoking conversation.

HELPING A PARTNER

When you are out there mixing it up with the enemy, one of the best kinds of protection you can have is a comrade-in-arms. Having a "teammate" of some sort—a spouse, a roommate, a best friend, or a close business associate—to help you navigate the room can be a godsend.

I don't mean that you and this partner should stay together at the event. Even under normal mingling conditions it's never a good idea to remain at the side of your spouse or your roomie when you go to a party; you will both have a much better time if you split up—you will ultimately meet and talk to more people that way. But when you are mingling with the enemy, it is even more important that you circulate separately, because that way you can assist each other. There are two main methods to support your teammate: you can help them avoid potential danger areas, and you can rescue them when they get into trouble.

Reconnaissance

Going to a party with a partner is like having a coconspirator. By checking in with each other from time to time throughout the party, you can warn each other about any mingling minefields you may have discovered. You can point out that pedantic pros-elytizer or drunk demonizer you just managed to escape from, so the other person won't have to go through the same torture you just did.

For instance, you might say, "Watch out for that guy in the red jacket over by the window seat; he's an avid Trump lover." Or "Be careful about talking to that curly-haired blonde woman in the corner, she's a super-militant vegan." Since you will obviously know what your partner's beliefs and level of tolerance are, you can act as their own social aide-de-camp.

Warning: Be very careful when whispering to each other about other people at the party. You definitely need to be discreet.

Rescue Mission

Many couples have prearranged signals they give each other from across the room when they want to be rescued from someone. Please don't try anything too obvious or odd like tapping the top of your head. It should be something like a tug on your ear, the fingering of your collar, or the adjusting of your glasses. Of course, your teammate has to be paying attention in order to notice; you may have to adjust those glasses for *quite* a while. If you need something more overt, you could try dropping a utensil on the floor (as long as there's no carpet). I know one woman who uses a certain kind of laugh—a loud one that is unnatural to her—to alert her wife.

When you show up for the rescue operation, you will need to be prepared to enter the group and introduce a new subject, or— if it seems necessary—remove your partner from the conversation entirely by taking their arm and saying, "Honey, sorry to drag you away, but I promised so-and-so I would introduce you." Then, with a quick smile and a nod, you are both away.

LENDING A HOSTING HAND

When you are the host you have a special responsibility to help things go smoothly. To ensure that everyone at your event has a good time, you naturally want to keep negative interactions (aka fights) to a minimum. While you never want to be too controlling, when guests feel their host is looking out for them, it actually makes them more relaxed.

To keep the peace, a good host will utilize many of the other techniques in this chapter. But a host should do even more. The host is the party coach, the captain of the ship, the director of the show. As such, the host needs to lay good groundwork and then keep an eye out to make sure things don't go awry. This does not mean either encouraging or discouraging weighty discussions; it just means making sure bottles are not going to be thrown at someone's head. The host needs to set the tone and then pay attention to make sure everyone has an enjoyable—or at least stimulating—time.

Guess Who's Not Coming to Dinner

Sadly, it's a fact that more and more parties, with the exception of business functions, are becoming "tribal"—that is, made up of only like-minded guests. A lot of people are afraid that getting Republicans and Democrats together at a party (on purpose) is tantamount to mixing oil with water, or fire with gasoline. Moreover, many people have said to me, "But I don't even *know* anyone from the other side!"

We are not to the point yet where people are asking to see guests' voter registration cards before they can enter your home. Certainly I believe that to avoid inviting someone to your party because that person has vastly different politics than most of the other guests is not the kind of impulse that is good for our society. We need to mix it up a little more often.

One thing to remember is that there is safety in numbers. If you invite sixty people to your open house, folks can fend for themselves quite well; with so much choice it's easy enough for a guest to engage in or avoid specific conversations. On the other hand, if you are having a dinner party of eight, you do need to curate the guest list. Dinner parties are more likely to engender political debate, which can be both good and bad. Inviting extremely volatile people who are on opposite political sides is a recipe you do not want served at your table. Of course, sometimes things are beyond your control; your friend's new boyfriend could be a highly opinionated and unexpected "enemy" element in your coterie. We don't always know everything about our guests—and what would be the fun of that?

I've had perfectly successful parties that included people of different persuasions. However, to be honest, I have not had the occasion to mix any outspoken Trump supporters with hardcore Bernie fans. I don't know how well that would work. Probably it would be disastrous. However, if people are respectful and intelligent I believe anything is possible. As the host, you have to guide people.

Host Treaties

It is sometimes not a bad idea to (playfully) give your guests a mandate about not arguing. As host, it is within your purview to get an agreement of one sort or another from your guests, a promise to keep their tempers in check. Sometimes, depending on your relationships and the level of partisan fervor of the guest(s), you might even tell someone at the time you are inviting them that there will be a guest of another color at your party (meaning blue or red) and that they should only come if they think they can behave. Or that one of the other invitees is particularly sensitive about a particular issue and you would be grateful if they didn't bring it up.

In the event of a combustible group—especially if you have sensed a contretemps in the making while you were serving the before-dinner drinks—you might deliver one of the following instructional lines at the start of your dinner, when everyone is seated:

> *"As a favor to me, let's not argue about politics tonight, people. Inside voices only!"*

> *"Let's make a deal. Gracie and Ted won't talk about how they hate Trump if Bill and Alice don't talk about how they hate Hillary. I want a promise from you guys. Okay?"*

> *"Just so you know, people who argue at my table don't get dessert."*

The Matchmaker and Matchbreaker

The best hosts are skilled at knitting people together during the event—figuring out which people are likely to be a good conversational fit as well as knowing when it may not be beneficial for certain people to be conversing together for too long. Connecting people is a host's ultimate goal. While the food and ambience are certainly important elements, most people agree that the real success of a party has to do with the quality of the conversation. Hosts should use what they know about the guests' temperaments, their interests, and their belief systems to help meld people in order to promote great conversations. But a host is responsible for "matchbreaking" as well as "matchmaking."

If you are hosting and you see any guests who seem to have steam coming out of their ears, you might go over to them and cheerfully say, "Okay guys. We're not going to solve the world's problems in one night." Or bring someone else into the conversation: "Excuse the interruption, but—Joe, have you met my cousin?" Stay there in that clique of people long enough to make sure it is moving along in a better direction before you leave. Another great host tactic to break up a fight is to ask one of the combatants to help you in the kitchen, or help you in picking out a Pandora station. Of course, the host can also use one of the subject-changing techniques outlined in chapter six—techniques that also come in handy if you are hosting a sit-down dinner and a political conversation is turning ugly. And in a pinch, you can always say, "I never allow people to argue at my table on days of the week that end in a Y."

The host of a social gathering should be like a gardener who is carefully tending all the plants and flowers, watering here and there to make sure things are growing, pulling up harmful weeds here and there when necessary. A respectful disagreement about politics is to be helped along and nurtured; a toxic conversation should be squelched.

Always take the high road,
it's far less crowded.

—Warren Buffet

CHAPTER EIGHT

When Mingling Online

Speaking of toxic conversations, I think most people can agree that society's biggest "fail" as far as human interaction goes is what is happening online. Social media sites seem to be where the greatest polarization is taking place, and where the two separate versions of reality are most prevalent. Social media is, ironically, one of the major *causes* of social discord at the same time that it is the place we most *experience* that social discord.

The internet has made it possible for us to connect with each other with the speed and in quantities that would have been beyond anyone's imagining a couple decades ago. Although by the time this book is published these numbers will have undoubtedly increased, the latest statistics show that Facebook has 1.4 billion daily users and generates 4 million gigabytes of data each day,[10] that there are 500 million tweets posted daily,[11] and that 95 million photos and videos are uploaded on Instagram per day.[12]

Many neuroscientists are studying the addictive nature of social media. Most believe there is a dopamine reward that occurs when people push and receive "likes" and "follows," and that platforms like Facebook, Snapchat, and Instagram take advantage of the same neural circuitry used by slot machines and cocaine to keep us hooked. In his book *The Organized Mind*, Daniel Levitin—referring to experiments involving the portion of the brain driving the limbic system—writes, "Each time we check a Twitter feed or Facebook update, we encounter something novel and feel more connected socially (in a kind of weird impersonal cyber way) and get another dollop of reward hormones." In general, if addiction is part of a motivational equation, it is not usually a good sign.

That social media sites—as well as other avenues of cyber-communication—are not particularly conducive to meaningful exchanges is not earth-shattering news. But it bears repeating because the amount of political discourse on social media continues to increase exponentially, without any signs of slowing down. Of course, the vitriol and outrage are not limited to Facebook, Twitter, and Instagram. Anywhere there is an online comment thread—from New York Times articles to YouTube videos—there are almost always escalating debates that devolve into petty personal attacks and acrimony.

To my mind, the biggest problem with online conversations is the lack of actual human contact. Trying to connect with people by posting online is like trying to paint a painting in a dark room, or trying to dance the waltz in snow boots. Letters on a screen are not enough. In an experiment carried out by UC Berkeley and University of Chicago researchers a few years ago, 300 subjects either read, watched videos of, or listened to arguments about controversial topics like war and abortion.[13] Afterward, the subjects were interviewed about their reactions to the opinions with which they disagreed. Guess what? People who had only *read* the commentator's words were more likely to label the speaker as ignorant or heartless than the ones who listened to or watched someone *say* those words. For me, one of the takeaways from this experiment is that without any nonverbal human signals to help contextualize a comment, what you write—or post—can be more easily misinterpreted. This is why the most innocent online comment can be misconstrued and can start an avalanche of angry replies or tweets.

If we were limited to having arguments face to face, we would all be a lot less divisive. However, people are not going to stop having fights on Twitter or Facebook because I say so. We can hope that social media sites themselves will improve—and indeed many are taking steps to do so—however, our best bet is to get wiser about how to use them.

HOW TO DON YOUR VIRTUAL ARMOR

People are becoming more social media-savvy every day, and I do think it might still be possible to eventually turn the ship around, to change the destructive course social media seems to be taking. I think as more and more people become aware of how these sites are affecting us, there will be corrections made—either by governments or in the marketplace—so that more options for healthier online venues will become available. There are already more sites emerging that are better at creating an atmosphere where hate speech and fake accounts are more effectively discouraged (ChangeAView.com for example). But we also need to be better, smarter consumers of the sites most of us use now.

When you go on sites like Facebook and Twitter, you should be using these spaces, they should not be using you (any more than they already do by collecting all your personal information to sell to big data companies). If you use it carefully, social media can be a place to be exposed to new ideas and opinions, as well as a great place for getting news from around the world. However, whenever you are "mingling" online, you need to stay emotionally centered, to carry with you onto the site a determination not to react viscerally to things you come across. Don't follow people without checking out their profile to see who they are; fake accounts and serious rabble-rousers are often easy to spot. Don't let yourself be drawn into discussions you later wish you hadn't. Seek out those accounts you have found to be informative or fun in the past, rather than just letting the site's feed dictate what it wants you to see. If there are people who routinely push your emotional buttons in a nonconstructive way, block them or hide them. (You can hide them without their ever knowing.)

I'm embarrassed to admit that sometimes, when I am trying to stay focused on writing or some other task, but need to go on social media for a minute just to check something or respond to something specific, I actually put my hand up between my face and the screen to block where I know the feed will appear. This way I don't have to see anything extraneous, and I can quickly navigate to where I want to go without getting drawn into something else that will take my attention. (Anyone watching me do this might think I was trying to ward off evil spirits—and maybe I am!)

I am not suggesting that you tune out opinions that are different from yours; on the contrary, we need to expose ourselves to differing points of view much more than we do now. What I am suggesting is that you be active rather than passive on these sites. Figure out how to actively seek out the things you want, when you want; don't let the site control you. Do not let yourself get sucked into arguments because they seem exciting, or because you think *I can't let them get away with this!* Most people who post heated political commentary never change their minds, and you are not going to convince them. Moreover, any comment you make on their post increases the likelihood that their future posts will appear at the top of your feed. Donning your virtual armor means that you stay aware of where you are and are prepared to not allow the posts—whether they are from strangers or acquaintances—to upset you. You are entering into a strange and vast virtual land. There are both comrades and monsters there. Tread carefully.

Of course, you may be one of the millions of people who would never think of engaging in a debate about politics online. The problem is that quarrels can, and often do, happen inadvertently. You start off posting about what you did over the weekend. You mention the great dinner you had with your girlfriend. Before you know it, you are trying to defend yourself from someone who is blaming you for the planet's greenhouse gas because you mentioned you had the veal.

SEVEN RULES TO POST BY

If you *are* someone who enjoys engaging in political discourse online, I would like to suggest that you follow a few rules. While it's challenging for people to learn to treat each other with dignity and respect online when our national leaders are setting such a bad example on social media, society will eventually disintegrate if we do not try to adhere to some basic standards of civility. Here are my seven rules to keep in mind when posting online:

1. **Consider your motives.**

   Before posting a political opinion, ask yourself, *Why am I posting this? Is it useful to others in some way or just about my own ego?* Are you adding anything new to the conversation? If you are posting only to support another person, and you are not adding anything new to the conversation, is it at least positive and/or helpful? Or does it just add to the noise?

2. **Be civil.**

   Don't be unkind or contemptuous. Even in the face of hate speech. Do not stoke the flames of anger or participate in public shaming. Never engage in personal attacks—name-calling or insults. There can be great temptation to do this because it can garner more online attention. However, mean-spirited communication is ultimately nonproductive and ends up hurting you as much as it hurts other people. As much as possible, show kindness and respect when dealing with others. Criticize the opinion, not the person. Emotional correctness is as important as political correctness. Remember this golden rule: Tweet others as you would like to be tweeted.

3. **Stay in the gray.**

    Avoid being an absolutist. Try not to share or post opinions that are completely black and white. Admittedly, with some issues, that's hard. Plastic bags are definitely hurting the environment; everyone agrees on that. But what I mean is, don't post things like "Anyone who has ever gone shopping without a tote bag is an enemy of the planet Earth."

4. **Know what it is and where it's going.**

    Don't retweet or post without knowing what it is you are posting. (Always read the article you are sharing or retweeting, and be cognizant of the website it came from.) And who is your audience? Who will see this post? Think before you click.

5. **Watch your font.**

    If you feel the urge to post using all caps, PLEASE DON'T! SHOUTING NEVER HELPS ANYTHING!! (Unless you are shouting for joy.) Ditto with the exclamation points. One or two is usually enough for any post.

And okay, using one word in caps is sometimes accept-able. But that's IT!

6. **Check your facts.**

   Consider the source. Be a discerning commenter. A 2018 study by researchers from M.I.T. found that falsehoods on Twitter were 70 percent more likely to be retweeted than accurate news.[14] So don't just think, *Hey, I always thought that sounded right, and now they've proved it. Time to share!*

7. **Limit your time on social media.**

   Set boundaries for yourself just as you do when you are watching your drinking or your sugar intake. Think about what your life goals are. Life is short; how much time per day do you want to spend typing and liking and scrolling down a screen?

COUNTING TO TEN (HOURS)

"Count to ten" was probably one of the best pieces of advice our parents or teachers gave us. The idea was that you were supposed to count to ten before you responded in anger, so you didn't say something you couldn't take back. But I don't think that's enough of a pause anymore, considering the level of outrage, stress, and lack of impulse control we have when we are on the internet. So I say: count to ten hours.

Counting to ten hours is another way of saying "sleep on it." Now I realize it is almost impossible to do this with social media—because for one thing everyone gets that FOMO (fear of missing out) feeling if they step away from the conversation that is unfolding in real time—but it is doable, and is especially advisable for emails and texts in situations where you are reacting in anger. So many unnecessary fights have happened by email or text. We hear about them all the time.

"I couldn't *believe* the email I got from my friend," someone will tell me. "I replied right away and told her I thought she was out of line, and that I had a lot on my plate right now, and she had a lot of nerve..." Of course, the other person was irritated and emailed back something even worse. It was days before they got it straightened out. We feel so justified in expressing every single thing we feel at the moment we feel it, partly because our devices make it so easy. If my friend had just waited until the next day—or even the next hour—before replying to that email, her whole week would have been easier, and the friendship wouldn't have sustained unnecessary damage.

Social media is not the only place we need to show restraint. Fights can escalate quickly when you are just messaging one-on-one. When you are upset, put your device down. If you want to type a response right away so you can get your thoughts down before you forget, fine, but then put it in your drafts folder or keep it in your Notes app until the next day. Or better yet, call the person the next day and have an actual conversation. The human voice is a beautiful and powerful communication tool that is not being used enough these days.

Actually, in our social lives, emailing is fast becoming extinct, having been almost entirely replaced by texting and direct messaging. Texting can be even more dangerous than emailing, because it is quicker. People are interacting with each other as fast as they can think—usually faster than they can even finish forming a sentence in their mind—and a response often comes back before the entire message is even sent. Just like talking, right? But remember you are *not* talking. There are no facial cues, no tone of voice to interpret. Unless the other person is about to board a plane for a country with no cell service, we need to slow down just a little and think before we type. We should all be against engaging in unprotected texts.

DEALING WITH TROLLS

Some people believe the internet term "troll" was originally a reference to the ugly dwarfs in Scandinavian fairy tales who were harmful to humans; other people believe it came out of the fishing term "trolling"—which is slowly dragging a baited hook from a moving boat. I don't think either origin for the term does justice to the level of damage a lot of these people are responsible for. Trolls are online users who start fights or disrupt conversations by posting inflammatory or insulting things, often off topic and meant to distract and anger people. People who just like to harass others online are also referred to as trolls. Trolls may target a particular person and cyberbully them mercilessly by bombarding them with venomous tweets or comments.

Some trolls are merely unhappy people who are spending too much time online; others may have a more malevolent, politically motivated agenda. They range from being a nuisance to being able to destroy people's lives. And, of course, some are not "people" at all but constructs of foreign governments trying to foment enmity and divide us against each other.

Disengagement

In certain cases, especially when you see someone else being subjected to cyberbullying, you might try to be of help by reporting the troll to the site's moderator. But for the most part, the best thing by far is to not engage. Avoid responding to a nasty, insulting comment or tweet. Don't even give the troll any satisfaction by telling them, "I'm blocking you." Just ignore them as though they do not exist.

Many online forums have a warning posted: *Please do not feed the trolls.* Now, most people know that not engaging with people who are mean-spirited or vicious is the smartest course of action, but sometimes it is hard to do. Many times trolls don't start off right away screaming insults at you, but they become more insulting as the conversation goes on. (Often the worst thing about them is that they make it impossible for you to continue a civilized conversation with other people on the thread.) However, as soon as you see this kind of behavior, ignore. Ignore, ignore, ignore. Don't give them their dopamine rush. Block them, hide them, delete them, or report them. Whatever you need to do. But do NOT engage.

Unless, of course, you are Sarah Silverman.

Making Miracles, or the Sarah Silverman Method

Sarah Silverman is a famous stand-up comedian and actress who is known for her appearances on *Saturday Night Live* and her Emmy-award winning show on Comedy Central. From 2017 to 2019 she hosted a late night show on Hulu called *I Love You, America*. She is fairly outspoken and often addresses controversial or taboo topics in her comedy.

In December of 2017, a story about the way Silverman dealt with a Twitter troll went viral. In response to a political tweet of the comedian's, a man tweeted a one-word slur on her feed: the "C" word. What Silverman did in response was extraordinary. Instead of reacting the way most of us would, in hurt or anger, or by simply ignoring him, she checked out the man's past tweets by looking at his feed, and gleaned enough about his life and circumstances to be able to reach out to him. She then tweeted:

"I believe in you. I read ur timeline & I see what ur doing & your rage is thinly veiled pain. But u know that. I know this feeling. Ps My back Fucking sux too. see what happens when u choose love. I see it in you."

They began an online conversation, during which he opened up to her, sharing details about his childhood abuse, his current financial struggle, and his back pain. He ended up apologizing to her, and she in turn enlisted the help of some of her twelve million followers to help him get medical help for his back. Silverman had basically killed the troll with kindness. She had responded to a hateful comment with compassion and had found common ground. She never forgot it was a fellow human being who had typed that comment. The next day the man tweeted out:

"God I feel so overwhelmed with joy tears in my eyes because I'm finally getting the help I need. Sarah Silverman is a complete angel. I'm in shock man shit like this never happens. I won't take it for granted."

After the story went viral, Silverman posted a tweet that included this sentence: "A bit embarrassed by the glory I'm getting from being human 2 another human. Literally everyone can do this." And she's right, of course. Wouldn't it be an amazing world if everyone did?

Sarah Silverman, you are my Twitter hero.

If you want to change the world, go home and love your family.

—Mother Teresa

CHAPTER NINE

Channeling Your Inner Buddha: Family Get-Togethers

Immensely amplified since the 2016 presidential election, the partisan-fueled fear of Thanksgiving dinner has by now become a trope. The dread of having political discourse with family during holidays has been so widely written about that it's now as proverbial as commercialism and Christmas. But with the country divided almost exactly in half, the danger of politics affecting your family relationships is no joke. In a 2016 Reuters/Ipsos survey, 15 percent of the respondents said they had stopped talking to a family member or close friend as a result of the election.[15] A November 2018 CBS News poll found that 40 percent of Americans were hoping to avoid talking about politics over Thanksgiving dinner.[16] Yet another study revealed that the 2016 election actually changed the length of Thanksgiving dinners that year; people who spent the holiday with relatives who voted for the opposite party cut their visit by thirty to fifty minutes compared to the year before.[17]

There are many reasons these familial encounters can be so daunting. Even without the element of politics, family visits are often stressful. After all, there is already enough to argue about: "Should the football game be on during dinner?" "Who didn't turn on the oven?" "Can't you remember after all these years that my daughter is allergic to nuts?" Families can provide our biggest joys but also present our biggest challenges. Every conversation you have is influenced by your past experiences together, including your past conflicts. There is so much history, so many childhood wounds festering beneath the surface. You may feel, consciously or not, a wistfulness that things should be the same as they once were, or a longing that they might have been different in the past. Your particular family dynamic, or power structure, is always at play in any discussion.

People are often deeply disappointed that others in their family do not think the way they do. It can be disturbing when siblings you were raised with have a completely different way of seeing things. It makes you feel the ground beneath you is shaky, and it can often seem almost like a betrayal. (And in the case of in-laws, it can put a strain on a couple's relationship.) When someone in your family voices an opinion that you believe to be totally wrongheaded, deluded, or even immoral, it's much worse than hearing an acquaintance say it. It's as if the body snatchers have come and replaced your family member with a pod person.

Dr. Jay Van Bavel, Associate Professor of Psychology at NYU, conducts research that examines how collective concerns—group identities, moral values, and political beliefs—shape the mind and brain. "The stakes are much higher when we disagree with our family members—these are people we've lived with and are often stuck with for decades to come," he told me.

The growing political "us and them" feeling seems to be undermining our family identity. But why are we so intent on sticking with our political "tribe" no matter what? "The reason is that our political identities fulfill a number of important motives—they give us a sense of belonging, status, and morality—which make them important to defend," said Dr. Bavel. "Unfortunately, these motives are often more powerful than our desire to find the truth or get along with others. We start to identify with a political party more than our other identities—like brother, colleague, or American."

Most people have one simple solution to the family visit: they don't discuss politics when they know that their relatives are on the opposite side. However, no matter what your intention is when you walk in the door, this is not always possible, because—as we know all too well—any and all conversations can lead to politics. And furthermore, if we avoid the important subjects, what does that solve in the end? How can we read the paper together every morning at breakfast and not mention what's in it? If we never discuss anything, our divisions will just get more solidified as the years go by.

This is not just about Thanksgiving dinner, which is, after all, only one day of the year. The challenges surrounding socializing with politically opposed relatives come into play at weddings, funerals, graduations, birthdays, reunions, summer vacations, and many more types of get-togethers, depending on how geographically (and emotionally) close families are. So is making politics a taboo subject really the only answer—that is, to stop talking to our dearest relatives about anything more important than who gets to eat the drumsticks this year, how tall the kids have gotten, and how nice the backyard looks?

You already know your family well, and you probably know where most of the landmines are. With family, you can't necessarily use the same strategies you would when you are mingling at a party of friends and acquaintances. While some techniques contained in the rest of this book do apply to your family get-togethers, many will not. Some of the methods below are modified versions of techniques in other chapters. However, since mingling with the family can be so difficult, it is worth putting these strategies in the right context here.

PRE-VISIT INSTRUCTIONS

In these situations—ones containing the double whammy of family relationship and political opposition—your mindset is extremely important. It's vital you prepare emotionally before you go. What do you think most people get therapy for anyway? Surviving family holidays, of course!

Staying loving, open-minded, and positive is the goal.

Start from Zero

Except for being aware of where the basic conversational pitfalls exist among your family, try to forget the conversations you've had in the past. In other words, don't arrive at the dinner with incontrovertible talking points to slay your uncle with because of a conversation you had last time. Don't let the upsetting altercation you had with him before color your upcoming conversation. This can be extremely difficult, I know. Sometimes the hurt and fear from what you perceived as an attack will stay with you and cause you to anticipate the same thing and/or want a do-over. And that very anticipation will make a fight more likely to actually happen.

The key is to try to start from scratch. Leave the past arguments behind. Just because the previous summer your sister went off the rails about transgender bathrooms, that does not mean she's spoiling to fight about it now, nor should it lead you to presume anything in particular about what she currently believes about other issues. One of the many problems of the "otherizing" trend is that we lump everyone and everything into two simple boxes. I know Republicans for whom protecting the environment is a key issue. I know Democrats who support gun rights and an increase in military spending. I know millennials who eschew smartphones and Baby Boomers who become hysterical if they are without theirs for ten seconds.

Don't assume you know what will happen in a conversation. You can't always predict. It's possible the brother who yelled at you last time about marriage equality regrets what he said. Or at least how he said it.

Commit to Curbing Your Alcohol Consumption (No, Really.)

I think many of us have learned this from experience. When you arrive at your family's home, your first thought may be that you need to drink more heavily than you ordinarily do. Naturally, you believe it will ease the tension and put you in a better mood, so that potential provocations will just roll right off your back. After all, isn't it better to be as relaxed as possible? To lower your stress? And anyway, perhaps you've had a long trip and a stiff drink seems just the thing.

The problem is, the main effect of alcohol consumption is that it lowers your inhibitions. As in, impulse control. So that when your cousin suddenly says something to you that you find objectionable, rather than being able to process it internally the way you know you should (*I don't hate this person, I just hate this idea. I know that people have different points of view, don't freak out, it's okay…*), the fact that you are a little tipsy may make you skip right to saying out loud, "That's just totally insane. You actually believe that crap?"

Be Prepared for Surprise Attacks

As I said, most people these days do not plan on engaging in political discourse with their opposite-party relatives. But accidents can happen, and explosions can erupt from the most unlikely, farthest corners of the conversation.

One Christmas years ago, I was singing one of my favorite funny holiday songs for the entertainment of my family. The song is an irreverent spoof on the "Twelve Days of Christmas" and contains lyrics like "The second day after Christmas, I pulled on the old rubber gloves, and very gently rung the necks, of both the turtle doves." I had sung this song before, and though my family usually teased me about being a ham and a showoff, they always enjoyed it. (Anyway, that's my story and I'm sticking to it.)

What I didn't realize was that I had never actually sung the song when my aunt was present. My aunt was a super-zealous animal rights person (in fact, when she died she left almost all her money to the ASPCA). I had no idea this song would offend her, but the issue of protecting animals was so important to her that she thought in singing this song I was being callous, and she interrupted me angrily after a few verses. An unpleasant couple of minutes ensued. I tried to convince her that my performance had nothing to do with animal rights, that it was just a silly parody. (No animals were harmed during the singing of this song!) But the song was just the catalyst, or tipping point, for her. She was a long-time vegetarian—she had been one since the early 60s, way before anyone else—and had been watching us all eat meat for years and saying nothing about it. This incident started a heated debate about meat eating. I guess you could say this was the song that broke the camel's back.

Stay alert. By this I don't mean you should not relax during your holiday dinner. It's just that you never know how the political argument will emerge, and you have to be ready to deal with it when it does. You may be really good at avoiding the subjects of Trump or health care, but then a conversation will take an unexpected turn and all at once you find—my late aunt should excuse the expression—that your goose is cooked.

Practice Psychic Self-Defense

Ultimately, you are always in control of whether you are in a state of love/hope or anger/fear. You cannot control what other people say. Everyone from the Dalai Lama to Oprah will tell you that your negative emotional reactions to what your family says are an extension of your own fear, your own issues.

Besides the years of therapy all of us need and rarely get, there are simple spiritual or psychological methods to help protect yourself. Some experts recommend the visualization trick of imagining a cocoon of white light or a thick white blanket around you, something that protects you. I once went to a healer who told me, among other things, to wear red socks whenever I was entering a potentially contentious interpersonal situation; the socks were supposed to ground me. And believe it or not it worked. Why did it work? Probably because I believed it would, or more to the point, the red socks just made me concentrate on staying centered. They were a reminder that I was going to endeavor to be my best, my kindest, and my wisest self.

LOVE MEANS NEVER HAVING TO SAY YOU'RE SORRY (THAT YOU VOTED FOR SOMEONE ELSE)

There is a belief among many people that if you don't challenge people whose views are "wrong," you are complicit in allowing those views to persist. That if we let things slide, nothing will change. This may be true under some circumstances. But not at your Thanksgiving dinner. Your goals are different when you are connecting with family.

Think about what your long-term goals are for these relationships. Every conversation you have is a building block in the construction of your lifelong intimacy. There's no rule that says you need to talk politics; for many people the decision to not talk politics with certain family members is the right one. They've tried it before; they know exactly what will happen. The definition of insanity is doing the same thing over and over and expecting a different result, and in some families it is simply insane to try to engage in these conversations—never mind reach any common ground.

If you are one of the people committed to NOT talking politics, what's the best way to still have meaningful exchanges, and not just talk about surface things? And how do you keep things from blowing up?

Positive Memory Sharing

This is a little bit like the technique in chapter four where you imagined the other person as a three-year-old. Almost everyone has wonderful memories of family members from the past—memories they cherish. Have some of these at the ready. Pack them up with you before you travel as you are packing your socks and underwear. During your car, plane, or train ride, think back to those memories you had with your relative(s). Remember the laughter and the love.

Later, over dinner with your family, if you sense the conversation is heading in the wrong direction, bring up one of these memories as quickly as you can. If the celebration is in your own home, you can suggest playing old videos or sharing childhood photos of fun vacations. This will help keep things in the love mode, which is where you want them.

Sometimes these shared memories can be of very small, funny moments in your past that you all remember—and have rehashed or recounted many times before—which is why they can work instantly to dispel a looming storm. Most families have memories relating to silly or absurd moments that will still make everyone laugh, sometimes until tears come down their faces.

For example, my father, who was a musician, was well known for his tendency to drift off into space, to let his mind wander so that he seemed completely unaware of what was going on around him. We used to tease him lovingly about this trait. ("Uh-oh, Dad's off in music land," we would say.) One evening years ago as we were gathering on the back porch for a summer dinner, we noticed my father was sitting and staring at his spoon, which he was holding in his hand. The rest of us were talking and passing food. Of course, he wasn't even seeing the spoon, he was off in music land. We all looked at him sitting there staring fixedly at the spoon as though he was trying to figure out what it was.

I leaned forward and touched his hand. "*Ssspoooonnnnn,*" I said to him in an exaggerated manner, as though he were a tiny child and I was teaching him how to talk. "SPOOONN!" With that, he snapped out of it, greatly abashed, and all of us laughed for about five whole minutes. Admittedly this is a very silly anecdote, but the point is that ever since then when there is tension at our family table, sometimes someone will only have to say, "Ssspooonnn…" and those of us who remember the story will crack up. A lot of families have shared-memory moments like this one.

Instead of invoking a memory or a family joke, you might threaten to tickle people, squirt them with water, or revert to other silly things you did when you were all younger. Any kind of lighthearted reminder that you had fun in your past. Obviously, all families are different, and what works for one may not work for another.

Ask for Help or Advice Instead of Discussing Beliefs

Let's say you are in the middle of dinner, and you are happily talking to your nephew about your new apartment in a city you've just moved to. Suddenly your father-in-law barks at you, "So you're moving to that city full of damn liberals, does that mean you are now one too?"

You don't have to take the bait. Instead you can quickly switch into advice-asking mode. "Yes, I'm moving next week," you might say. "By the way, do you know anything about moving a piano? My mover won't do it." Or "Do you have any advice about the best way to go about finding a new dentist there? I won't know anyone yet and I don't want to just look one up online."

You can ask your brother's husband about buying a new computer, ask your mother about recipes, ask your father about gardening. Everyone likes feeling needed.

Magic Talisman: The Family Pet

I have heard a lot of great stories about pets influencing our social lives. Animals can be incredibly helpful as a diversion or smoothing-over device when things get heated. One of these memorable incidents took place during a large family Christmas dinner of a friend of mine. According to this friend, an argument had begun to brew between the sister of the host (let's call her "Sis") and the host's wife ("Mrs. Host"). Someone at the table had mentioned the difficulty of figuring out travel details and vacation time when Christmas happened to fall on a Wednesday.

"I don't know why Christmas Day should even *be* a national holiday when the Jewish and Muslim holidays are not," complained Sis, who had a predilection for starting family fracases.

"For god's sake, Jewish and Muslim holidays are often not one-day holidays," retorted Mrs. Host. "We can't close down the country for a whole week, or a month. And besides, the majority of the people in America are Christians. I can't stand this left-wing attack on Christmas."

Someone else chimed in: "What about the division of church and state? Why should *any* religious holiday be a national holiday?" Soon half the table was yelling.

In the middle of this melee, the family dog, an old pug, came tearing down the stairs to see what the fuss was all about, barking at the top of his little lungs. Everyone turned to look at him; as he neared the bottom he lost his footing and tumbled down the last few steps, head over paws. After it was apparent the dog was okay, the table erupted in laughter and the fight was over.

While you can't count on this kind of perfect timing, a pet really is like a magic wand or a secret weapon. If there are pets present at Thanksgiving dinner, you are way ahead of the game.

At the first hint of trouble, you can declare, "Where did that cat Spooky get to?" Or "Hey! Where's my cutie-pie little doggie?" Or, "What the heck is that crazy Buddy doing?" Look for the dog, praise the dog, ask after the dog's health. Get the dog to do tricks. And if things are really bad, go out and walk the dog.

In fact, if you don't own a pet, I highly suggest getting one before the next holiday season rolls around.

DIVIDE AND CONQUER (OR AT LEAST CONTAIN)

When you do feel like having a meaningful conversation about an issue with a family member, it is best not to try it at the dinner table, with everyone watching and listening. When talking to a passionate opposite-party relative, you are going to do better one-on-one than in a group, where this relative (and maybe you) might have something to prove, or family status to win or lose. Often if you can get this person away and have a quiet moment together—going out to get wood, going to the store for last-minute supplies—everyone's guard will be down. When it's just two of you, you are either bonding over the task at hand or perhaps reminiscing about something special between you. Some of my best and deepest conversations about important things took place when I was fishing with my father, just the two of us.

When you are off taking part in an activity together, you are establishing what I think of as a relationship "cushion"; you are having a constructive familial moment. Sometimes it can lead to a surprising breakthrough, where one or the other, or both of you, starts to really listen and says, "I see your point, I really understand how you can feel that way." It is not a capitulation; it does not mean, "You are right and I am wrong." It is an acceptance of the other's state of mind, of whatever influences are playing on them. From there you might be able to go further in explaining your point of view next time.

Separating from the pack is a good way to lower the stakes and bond.

BABY STEPS: VENTURING OUT OF THE NEUTRAL ZONE

When you decide to venture into the political subject areas (which, let's face it, encompass much of what is interesting in the world), you are a braver man than me, Gunga Din, but there are some guidelines that will help you.

Remember, never concentrate on winning or changing someone's mind. Instead your aim should be a conversation in which each party understands more fully why the other holds a given belief.

This can be very challenging, but you must really let go of the need to prove the other wrong. Ask yourself, *Do I prefer to be right or have an interesting exchange?* You may feel that if you give up your judgment of what is right and wrong, your finely honed perception of the issues, that you are condoning the other person's position. And that if you don't tell them they're wrong, in no uncertain terms, then that means you're part of the problem. Just remember that not only is this not the UN, but also that anger is not a winning strategy. All it does is promote more anger on the other side. You react, they react, you react more strongly, and so on. Your only viable course of action is to try to listen to each other. Of course this is easier said than done. But remember what the Dalai Lama says: "If you want others to be happy, practice compassion. If you want to be happy, practice compassion."

We are not all spiritual masters. I'm not saying that it's possible to let go of all your anger in these situations. But sometimes it is better to release your anger in different ways, like after you have escaped to your bedroom and you can scream into your pillow.

Teach by Doing: Set an Example

I can't tell you how effective it is to simply behave in the manner you want others to behave. It's a cliché because it's true. Just try it and see. If you have the fortitude to change your behavior—to be kinder, and more respectful—it will cause others to follow suit. Maybe not instantly, but over time. While I was interviewing people for this book, I came across many excruciating stories of people whose father told them, "How could you vote for that person? You're not one of us!" or whose sister told them, "No sister of mine could be so stupid and mean." It would seem almost impossible to respond to those kinds of attacks with love or respect, but it can be done. And in fact, it is the only way to change that kind of energy.

Your mission, should you choose to accept it: No matter what anyone else does, you will show respect even when the other one doesn't. Here are your basic tenets:

* Communicate, don't attack.

* Talk about the issues; don't talk about particular politicians. (Once you start talking about Trump, it's all over.)

* Be curious about what the other people think, even though, after countless Thanksgivings, you are convinced you already know what they think.

* Never show contempt, *ever*. This can be hard in families, where you are used to not bothering to be polite the way you would with other people.

* Be grateful. Gratitude is powerful. It can transform situations. Thank your un-likeminded relative for anything you can think of: For making your bed up. For building a fire. For making the dessert. For complimenting your hair.

* Forgive. Learning to forgive is like learning a martial art; you have to practice to get better and stronger at it. Within families it can be essential for your future happiness. Forgiveness is an essential part of wisdom.

Your "Safe Word"

Sometimes, if you have a habit of getting into fights at family functions, but you still like to try to engage in political discourse, you might all affectionately agree on a safe word. A safe word is a word that all parties involved agree means that you stop the conversation, no matter what. The safe word should be something that is humorous or silly (banana split, harmonica, jellyfish, snickerdoodle) and therefore is more effective at snapping you out of negativity than one of you simply saying, "Let's not talk about this anymore."

Some companies use a more codified version of this method to ensure a safe office atmosphere. I know someone who works in an office where there was an employee seminar held in order to set forth guidelines about appropriate and inappropriate language. The person running the seminar told the employees that if any conversation seemed questionable or made anyone uncomfortable, they should use the terms "green light" (meaning this is fine, go ahead), "yellow light" (you're getting into an area I'm not that comfortable with), and "red light" (I don't want to talk about this).

The funny thing is that after the seminar the employees would use this code in a more or less ironic way. If they were sitting around having lunch and someone began talking about something the slightest bit politically incorrect, one person would shout, "Yellow light, yellow light!" and they would all laugh at the absurdity of having this kind of verbal alarm system and then continue on with the conversation. Still, they would usually proceed a little more carefully. The humorous version of this officially prescribed code worked as a tension releaser as well as a warning signal. If this stoplight code seems more suited to your family sensibility than using a silly word like "snickerdoodle," try it.

You have only two choices when it comes to facing your Thanksgiving dinner. Either avoid the subject of politics altogether, or converse with kindness and respect. Buddha taught that practicing loving-kindness was the antidote to fear. Confucius warned, "When anger rises, think of the consequences." Gandhi said, "Whenever you are confronted with an opponent, conquer him with love." Who are we to argue with all that?

If you have learned how to disagree without being disagreeable, then you have discovered the secret of getting along—whether it be business, family relations, or life itself.

—Bernard Meltzer

CHAPTER TEN

Handling Special Circumstances

There are some situations that, for one reason or another, fall outside of the regular "mingling with the enemy" territory—that is, political discourse during planned social occasions. After all, our social experiences extend into all our personal interactions. Whether it's a brief encounter with a stranger or an ongoing relationship with a person we come into contact with during our daily routine, we connect and converse with a myriad of individuals who are not in the category of friend, acquaintance, coworker, or relative. There's the conversation with your Uber driver or the interaction with the person in line with you at the store. There's the morning chat with your postal worker or the checkout clerk. There's the exchange you have with the person sitting next to you at the café or the bar, or on the train.

This chapter will include tips on dealing with strangers in public places as well as with the people you interact with regularly during the course of your life. Your exchanges may be brief with these individuals; however, for the sake of the quality of your life, it's still desirable that these peripheral interactions be positive experiences. In this chapter we will also discuss what to do when you are mingling at social events with an actual personal "enemy"—not just an ideological one—such as an ex from a bad breakup or someone who picked a fight with you at the last community meeting.

Lastly, while throughout this book I have been advising you to avoid fighting about politics at all costs, there are times when you will decide to face your enemy and—charge into battle. If you do happen to be someone who would rather not let outrageous or incendiary things go unchallenged, and like to get in there and mix it up, there is a right way and a wrong way to proceed.

But first, let's talk about mingling in public.

ADVICE FOR HANDLING UPSETTING PUBLIC ALTERCATIONS

Every time you leave your house and interface with strangers, there exists the possibility of having to navigate politically charged conversations. Riled up from talk shows and social media and intoxicated by the "us versus them" perfume in the air, a lot of people out there are ready for a fight. Tolerance is at an all-time low. It's hard enough when you are at a party, but when you are out there in unprotected arenas with total strangers, you are really flying blind. It can be onerous to deal with it when issues come up in public venues.

A friend of mine recounted a disconcerting experience she had while walking in a park recently with four or five friends. She was chatting with a woman named Tina—a friend's roommate whom she had just met that afternoon—when they happened to pass some male teens who were sitting on a bench, vaping.

Suddenly, right in the middle of a sentence my friend was uttering to her, Tina yelled over at the teens, "No vaping! It's against the law in a public park. You're going to get arrested!" Now technically, vaping, like smoking, is illegal in this particular park. However, my friend felt that the teens were not really bothering anyone, since they were outside and there was no discernable second-hand smoke. (E-cigarettes do produce second-hand vapor, but it is more subtle.)

What my friend did in response to Tina's sudden outburst was what many people would do. First, she tried to just ignore it and continue with the conversation they had been having. But Tina was now wholly focused on the teens, and kept shouting at them to stop vaping. They were getting angry and calling taunts back at her. My friend was embarrassed and also a little nervous that the interaction would escalate, so she walked quickly to join the other friends in the group who were walking a little farther ahead on the path. Tina continued to harangue the teens, who started shouting back more loudly. Eventually the "vapers" ran up ahead so that my friend, Tina, and the rest of her group had to pass by them again. "I'm telling you, you're going to be arrested, and vaping is not good for you!" Tina repeated. She would not let it go. Eventually the teens and my friend's group got far enough away from each other on the path that there was no further confrontation, but my friend told me it had marred the whole outing for her.

If you are a bystander to this kind of obviously over-the-top response like Tina's, the first thing you should do is try to dig down and find some empathy for her position on the issue, even when the confrontation itself may be unacceptable. Most of us have certain things that push our buttons, things that are our own personal bugaboos.

For instance, when I am at the beach I often visit in Delaware, I tend to go slightly postal when I see anyone feeding the seagulls French fries on the beach. First, it's not good for the birds; second, it's illegal, a fact that is posted on a big sign on the boardwalk, right beside the steps to the beach. Most important, tourists feeding the seagulls on a crowded beach create a feeding frenzy, so that if you are anywhere near them on the beach, you have hundreds of birds flocking around violently and pooping on your head. And yet, many people think it's adorable to let their toddlers feed the birds.

My family knows this is my particular pet peeve, so whenever we see someone feeding a seagull, they glance nervously at me, dreading the inevitable confrontation. "Oh, no, here she goes," one will say as I rise to my feet. The rest of the family puts towels over their faces in embarrassment, or takes this moment to get up and go for a swim.

I like to think I am not as abrasive about this infraction as the anti-vaping woman was with the teens. (My family might disagree.) It definitely annoys me, but I always try to be polite. However, because I know how upset I get about the seagulls, I try to be more forgiving about other people's hot-button issues.

What is the most helpful response in these kinds of situations? What I, and Tina, and others in these situations need to do first is to calmly inform the offending person about the rules. Give them the benefit of the doubt; they may not even know the rules, or have ever considered how the transgression affects others. Most people aren't really thinking about it. And most are perfectly okay with being told, if you are respectful and nonjudgmental about it. "I'm so sorry to interrupt you, but did you know you are not supposed to feed the seagulls on the beach/vape in the park?" is the proper beginning.

Of course, these are both relatively minor examples. Things can get much more out of control when you are in an enclosed space—like a bar or an airplane—or when the subject of contention is more political and is one that is already polarized and magnified by the media. We've all witnessed or read about people who go ballistic and have to be thrown off planes, tossed out of restaurants, or removed from stadiums. There are plenty of times when I am at a bar or restaurant with a friend, and the person sitting next to us overhears our conversation and decides to put in their two cents (which quickly turns into a dollar's worth). Often it starts off civil enough, but with an edge to it. If my friend and I are not careful to deflect the interloper, the situation can become uncomfortable—not to mention that it will disrupt the private conversation we are trying to have. These days people tend to have their ears peeled and their political dukes up.

This lowering of decorum has been happening for a while. "Values have changed," P.M. Forni wrote in his 2009 book, *The Civility Solution: What to Do When People Are Rude.* "Self-esteem and self-expression are in; restraint is, if not out, an annoying afterthought. When we lack restraint, we inevitably hurt others and eventually pay dearly ourselves." We don't only encounter the polarization at the office holiday party or our family Thanksgiving dinner, it's everywhere. We are on the alert all the time for people who might be on the other "team." This is why focusing on treating others with respect and civility is so important. "Incivility and violence are partners," says Forni. "When we manage to keep the level of incivility down, the level of violence decreases accordingly."

When you come across someone while you are out and about who seems contentious, you have to try to ascertain whether this is a person you want to engage with or not. When you are in public and someone picks a political fight with you, or any other kind of fight for that matter, the best thing is to—as subtly as possible—ignore or disengage.

More complicated, of course, is if you see someone else in trouble. In spite of the advice I offer in chapter seven about peacemaking, I recommend ignoring strangers who are having a loud argument when you are out in public, unless the fight seems headed for physical violence, and even then you should alert someone in authority rather than trying to step in yourself. It is never a good idea to become involved in these types of altercations, for obvious reasons—unless someone is getting physically beaten up, and you are six feet tall and/or have some training in self-defense (and there's no time to dial 911).

Of course the majority of the time you will not run into any trouble. I love talking to strangers, anywhere, anytime, and I have always found most people to be respectful and polite—as well as usually really interesting. But I do believe fuses are a bit shorter these days. Remember, it's the escalation of an issue that is always the danger. So while engaging with strangers out in the world can be fun and rewarding, stay clear of any ugly clashes that do not involve you, and try to resist adding fuel to any and all fires.

TANGLING WITH THE TANGENTIAL: DOCTORS, DOORMEN, AND DRY CLEANERS

Whether it's a conversation with a neighbor, a customer, your podiatrist, your hairstylist, your mechanic, or your mail carrier, you never know when you are going to find yourself in an awkward spot, conversationally. There are many people we come in contact with regularly; these peripheral social relationships can add greatly to the quality of our daily existence. I think of these as social side dishes in the smorgasbord that is our mingling universe. Most of the time we don't know what the political affiliation or ideologies of these people are. But especially since the

2016 election, everything has been kicked up a notch, and we are more likely to slip into treacherous topics before we realize it.

When You Are the Service Provider

I live in a building with a doorman and have talked to some of my doormen about how they stay out of heated political debates. I had assumed it would be pretty easy, because interactions with the tenants are usually fairly brief and frequently revolve around trivial matters. "No, it's sometimes really, really hard," one doorman confessed to me. "We have to be so careful. A lot of tenants want to talk about the president, and other things in the news. I have to walk a tightrope."

A lot of the peripheral relationships in our lives are transactional. That is, someone is providing a service to someone else as part of their making a living. The service providers can't afford to lose their cool; their livelihood depends on it. If you are a service provider, the general rule is to stay far away from politics unless you are absolutely sure it's not going to cause trouble. If you develop a relationship over time with someone, you will know when the conversational water is safe. But even then, you should be careful.

A person I interviewed told me she went to see an otolaryngologist she had never been to before, and when the subject of insurance came up (the patient was afraid a treatment might not be covered), the doctor said contemptuously, "Well, if we get Hillary, health insurance is only going to get worse." It doesn't really matter whether the patient agreed with the doctor or not. The point is, if you are a doctor, it's best not to offer up any political opinions unless you have known your patient for years and are darn sure she feels the same way.

My own hairstylist is so careful, he wouldn't even talk to me about the issue of having to be careful about talking to me! He's trained himself that well. He knows that even though it could start off fine, the conversation could hit a snag, and it could be bye-bye customer.

When You Are the Consumer or Customer

You should be just as careful if you are on the other side of the transaction—that is, if you are the customer, the client, or the patient. These types of relationships can include shopkeepers, delivery people, or people at the front desk where you work or at your gym. They can be people you chat with once or twice or folks you have to see all the time. These instances constitute some of the only times you have to *always* err on the side of abstaining from having any opinion. You don't know who the "enemy" is, nor do you want to. You cannot afford to alienate people in your daily life. If you want to, you can try testing for "friend, foe, or fanatic" (see chapter three, "Conversational Recon") and then proceed with caution, but it's safest to make sure the person is really on your side of the issue. And as I have said before, don't assume just because you know one or two things about the person's beliefs that you know how they feel about everything else.

Neighbors

Neighbors can also be very tricky. I'm not referring here to those neighbors who have become your friends; friends and acquaintances are covered in other chapters. But there is a reason most people are wary about socializing with their neighbors. Your neighbors are a more or less permanent part of your life. There is no question about whether or not you are going to see them in the future; you are almost definitely going to run into them now and again. When you befriend a neighbor you usually proceed slowly and carefully, because if it goes wrong somehow, you can't just say, "Well, I just won't see that person anymore." There is really no escape.

It's tempting to bring up politics with someone who lives near you, as you already feel somewhat connected by location. And of course, many times people who live in the same geographical area do, in fact, share the same political bent. But you just never know. It's imperative that you keep these relationships cordial. Once someone has left the elevator (or the neighborhood playground) in a fit of pique, it's hard to put the genie back in the bottle. You don't want to have an unpleasant exchange about politics with a neighbor and then find yourself hanging back in your building lobby to avoid having to ride up with that neighbor, or peering out your window to make sure they are not in their front yard when you go out to get the paper. Your home is your castle; you don't want it to turn into a foxhole.

As in all of the "tangential" situations above, my general advice concerning neighbors—as boring and inauthentic as it may sound—is to pretend you don't have a strong opinion, or even to pretend that you have no opinion. And if the neighbor starts expressing a viewpoint that sets your teeth on edge—just smile through those teeth as much as you can and end the interaction as quickly and politely as possible.

A WORD ABOUT FACING NONPOLITICAL "ENEMIES"

On the social battlefield, it's not just people who have different ideologies who can threaten your equilibrium. There are other kinds of "enemies." There are times you will find yourself at the same party as the colleague who stole an account from you, the boss who fired you, or just a person who has rejected your invitation to lunch for five years in a row. The woman who spurned your romantic advances last week could suddenly join a conversation you are in with two other people who are important to your professional life. A person who has insulted you in the past, or been really mean to a friend, could suddenly be standing next to you at the buffet table. Or you could suddenly run into a person with whom you have committed such a severe faux pas in the past that polite conversation seems an unreachable goal—that their very presence makes you want to run for the hills. Wait—the man who cursed violently at you for accidentally cutting in front of him at the box office yesterday—and now it turns out he's the guest of honor? *Awk-ward!!*

A woman I interviewed, Lilly, recounted a "mingling with the enemy" experience of this type that made her want to swear off parties forever. She had been invited to a birthday party for a relatively new friend of hers named Jennifer. While Lilly realized she would not know anyone there, she wanted to cement her friendship with Jennifer, so she screwed up her social courage and went. It was a backyard barbecue with about fifty people. After about twenty minutes, Lilly had introduced herself to two or three people and felt she was getting into the groove. Then Jennifer ushered a tall women over to her. "I wanted you to meet my friend Cecily Smith," said Jennifer. "I think her son Brian goes to the same school as your son." Lilly's heart stopped. Brian Smith was her son's nemesis. He had been bullying her son. All attempts at trying to communicate with Brian's parents had failed; they had had only one phone conversation during which the mother—this same woman now standing in front of Lilly holding a glass of white wine—had told her in no uncertain terms that her son was lying and Brian had never bullied anyone, that in fact it was Lilly's son who was the troublemaker. The two mothers exchanged a very stiff hello, and as soon as she could, Lilly made a hasty retreat—away from Jennifer and away from the party. Unfortunately, by leaving the party, Lilly missed out, unnecessarily, on meeting other people. And who knows, she and Jennifer may even have been able to begin to bridge the gap of misunderstanding between them.

The point is, whether it's that you suddenly realize you are chatting with someone whose politics are the complete opposite of yours or you happen to notice that your ex-boyfriend just entered the party on the arm of the person who stole him away from you, it can cause the same kind of social anxiety and can paralyze you.

Almost all the techniques I have described in this book are applicable to these nonpolitical situations. You need to be careful about assuming, try to find common ground if you can, and employ your subject-changing techniques and exit strategies if need be. However, when it's a personal situation rather than an ideological difference of opinion, the stakes can be higher and the challenge tougher. Your fear and anger in these situations are deeper, because it's personal. The good news is that sometimes a relaxed social situation can, believe it or not, actually be an unexpected healing opportunity for the combatants. Being face to face at a party might be uncomfortable at first, but if you talk about other things, you just might be able to connect with your enemy better than you might have imagined. In fact, compared to the personal animus that exists between you, talking politics might actually be a boon under these circumstances. Especially if you are on the same page politically, an engaging conversation about politics could get your mind off the bad blood between you.

On the other hand, if it turns out you are both political *and* nonpolitical enemies, you'll be in a combat zone of disastrous proportions and your only hope of survival will be hasty retreat (but not from the entire party, please, if you can help it).

PICKING BATTLES: WHEN IT *IS* WORTH A SKIRMISH

Throughout this book I have talked a lot about avoiding arguments. Since this is primarily a social guide, this has been my basic message: keep your discussion civil, or dodge. However, at the risk of contradicting everything I have said, the truth is that we are living in extraordinary times, and inevitably there will be moments that arise where you simply cannot let something pass by without challenging it, lest you feel you are being a coward or being untrue to yourself. In some cases, you may feel you have a moral or ethical duty to speak up.

As Marianne Williamson puts it in her book A *Politics of Love,* "What has happened in our country since the last presidential election makes political disengagement no longer an option for any serious person. We've learned the hard way the truth of the old French saying 'If you don't do politics, politics will do you.'"

Oftentimes, circumstances themselves will dictate whether or not you end up sparring about politics. Some get-togethers you attend will be made up of guests who are extremely politically engaged. On these occasions, the percent of political conversations (and potential disagreements) will be naturally higher. Especially if you are in your twenties, imparting your ideas to everyone you meet is probably going to be like breathing to you. Also, sometimes the nature of your profession makes it difficult to not discuss political issues wherever it is you happen to be, whether it's social or not. For example, I have a physician friend who is an award-winning reproductive rights activist, and it is virtually impossible for her to avoid talking about abortion and birth control once someone asks her what she does for a living. If your job is writing for a conservative think tank, working at the Pentagon, or lobbying for the NRA, the same thing might apply.

Moreover, in spite of what I have said about heated arguments ruining a party, sometimes placing harmony above all else can make a social event boring. It always depends on the temperament of the guests and the reason for the gathering, but if you have the right mix of smart people on opposite political sides at your dinner party, it can be quite invigorating, as long as no one throws anything. As Priya Parker, a strategic advisor trained in the field of conflict resolution, says in her thoughtful book *The Art of Gathering,* "Good controversy can make a gathering matter."

I have said I am against using sarcasm during political discourse, and so I am—for the most part. But one evening at my local pub I heard someone ranting to the person next to them about something political. I could not tell exactly what it was, but it had to do with the Mueller investigation. The person bearing the brunt of the rant did not say much, until finally he looked up at the other person and said mildly, "I sure wish they'd turn up the music. I can hear you too well."

I admit it; I got a serious kick out of that guy. (But reader, don't try this at home.)

Of course, that sarcastic remark was not meant to engender a discussion. That was an "I don't want to talk to you about this" remark. In contrast, should you make the decision to actually argue about your issue, once you are committed to promoting your point of view, it's advisable to follow the few guidelines I have outlined below. But first, let's look at one of the main motivations for a skirmish.

Them's Fightin' Words

There are some statements that people may make (though not often, one would hope) that many of us will not be able to let go without taking umbrage—either because the statements are so ridiculous or because they are so horribly offensive, or both. These are either walk-away-in-disgust lines or get-in-there-and-try-to-educate-the-person lines. I'm listing just a few examples below. I'm trying to be bipartisan here. Trigger warning for everyone!

Sample "fightin'" lines:

> "Most women who are raped could have avoided it by not dressing provocatively."

> "The Catholic Church has never done anyone any good, but has only caused harm."

> "The media is the enemy of the people."

> "Donald Trump is a war criminal and should be executed."

> "No cop ever shot an innocent person."

"All Republicans hate black people."

"No one who wears a head scarf belongs in Congress."

"It should be illegal to make more than ten million dollars a year."

When people are saying mean or hateful things, it can be excruciatingly difficult to remain unflustered and to respond with respect. Nevertheless, that is your goal. Remember, you do have the option of walking away from the person. However, you can also counter with, "I disagree wholeheartedly with that statement," and then, as calmly as you can, explain why.

Basic Training

Ideally, the dispute you are having will not involve any of the above hyperbolic pronouncements but instead will be at least a little more nuanced. There are hundreds of complex issues you might want to endeavor to debate with someone. No matter what the topic, you should try to keep in mind a couple of fundamental principles as you prepare to engage the enemy.

First, always remember your aim is to try to persuade the person, not insult them. If you can't persuade them (which is most likely going to be the case), you can at least attempt to present them with new information, expose them to a new point of view or way of thinking. Second, try not to allow your passion about the subject to override your logical arguments. Make sure you have your facts straight. It's important to note here that nowadays there is a relatively new impediment to intellectual debate: alternative facts. Never before has there existed such a dichotomy of realities; if two people can't agree on the basic facts about what is happening or has happened, it's almost impossible to have a debate about solutions. If you come up against this kind of factual brick wall, you may have to give up the fight before it starts.

However, if that is not that case and you are someone who is often compelled to enter into political debate at parties, it is worth studying up on the top ten or fifteen logical fallacies. A logical fallacy is an error in the logic of an argument that makes the argument invalid but does not prevent it from swaying people's minds. One example of a logical fallacy is something called the "straw man." In the straw man fallacy, your opponent attacks a position you don't actually hold. For example, your opponent might say, "Senator X wants to leave our country defenseless," when your actual position is that you support Senator X for not wanting to add any more money to the defense budget. Another type of logical fallacy is the "false dilemma," or "false dichotomy." This is an assertion based on erroneous reasoning and is an "either-or" type of argument. It's when someone presents only two choices, when in fact more choices exist, and claims that one is acceptable and the other is not. So someone arguing against the defunding of the National Endowment for the Arts might say, "You either love art, or you don't."

There are ten or fifteen of these common debate practices, which are easy to look up online. If you become familiar with them, they can be much easier to contend with when someone uses them in an argument. When you can see them coming, you can parry them more easily and can be more equable in your response.

Conscientious Objections

When you are in a conversation and you come up across a truly bad bump in the road—that is, the other person is espousing something that you feel is just so wrong you want to scream—don't roll your eyes, don't groan or cover your eyes with your hands. Avoid the three C's: contempt, condescension, and conceit. Instead, try using one of the following lines. If you practice these they will come in handy when you're starting to feel indignity or exasperation.

"Maybe there is a different way of looking at it."

"I wish I were as certain as you are."

"I'm afraid I can't agree."

"I agree with your premise, but I arrive at a different conclusion."

"I can understand how you feel. I feel a little differently."

"On the other hand, one could argue that..."

The Broken Record

Sometimes you can tire the other person out when they have really gotten going and are basically on a diatribe. Now that vinyl records are cool again, everyone will know what I mean by a broken record. Just like when the needle skips on the record, you repeat the same acknowledgment over and over until the other person runs out of steam.

"I understand what you are saying."

"Yes, I understand."

"Yes...I hear you."

"I get it."

Eventually the other person will probably get the message that they need to either stop and listen to you or move on to another point.

Know the No-No's

Here is a short list of things to avoid doing during your debate, if humanly possible:

* Try not to raise your voice. If you feel yourself getting angry, take a deep breath or two. Look away from your opponent for five seconds. Keep self-checking your voice volume.

* As tempting as it is when you feel there is a lot at stake in what you believe, try not to exaggerate to make a point, and don't use broad sweeping statements. Don't say things like, "Look, I've read everything there is to read about this, and let me tell you…" or "Come on, *everyone* knows that…"

* Don't get personal. Don't ever say anything like "What if it was *your* daughter?"

* Never make judgment statements, such as "You're living in a bubble," "You're wrong," or "You're part of the problem."

I know what some of you are thinking: They *are* part of the problem. Why shouldn't I tell it like it is? Why shouldn't I wake them up? But when mingling with the enemy, one of the worst things you can do is to attack the other person. You want to oppose their position, not them. The second you blame an individual for a political problem (unless of course they are holding a government office), the discussion is over and you have, in essence, lost.

When you feel the impulse—and it can be a strong one—to do any of the above, try to project a demeanor that is thoughtful and respectful, even if you have to "fake it till you make it." In other words, we can often trick ourselves out of our own outrage by acting "as if" (*as if* the person has not just said something morally reprehensible, or airheaded). It's a proven fact: Pretend to be in a good mood and you can trick yourself into it. Pretend that you are not horrified and it will mitigate your emotions. A fake-it-till-you-make-it attitude is one that will serve you well in many areas of your life but is especially applicable in these situations. At the very least it is a way of curbing yourself, of delaying things, before you say something you may later regret. Even just pretending to be respectful and compassionate will rub off a little—on you *and* on your enemies.

Emergency Mode: When There's Been a Recent Catastrophic Event

On the night after 9/11, I vaguely remember a violent argument two of my best friends had on the sidewalk about the idea of assassinating Osama bin Laden. An hour later, the same two people were crying and hugging each other.

When you attend a social event on the evening of, or weekend after, a national disaster or tragedy—whether it be a school shooting, an embassy bombing, or a devastating hurricane—everyone's nerves are on edge, and their views about the event, their political ideology, and any defensiveness they have about their beliefs will be at an apex.

Being angry is a natural and understandable response when people have lost their lives, but be careful not to misdirect this feeling. You may believe the person standing in front of you is in some way partly responsible because of how they voted or what their positions on the issues are, but remember that no one wanted this thing, whatever it was, to happen. (Unless you are mingling with a bona fide terrorist.) Hardly anyone is heartless. Some people are more self-involved than others; some people have tunnel vision because of their upbringing, their geographical location, or their profession. And yes, some people are a little selfish. But accusations (at a social event) will not help. Save it for the organized protest, for your action in the community or within the government.

All the admonitions involving not talking politics do not really apply on these occasions, because in these situations people are going to be talking about everything that has happened, as well they should. When people's emotions are raw, it's even more important for everyone to be their best self. Concentrate on emitting positive or loving energy when you are at an event held right after a major catastrophe.

As always, remember your ultimate goal: connection with your flawed, fearful, fabulous fellow human beings.

The "Enemy" Dispelled

In 2018, the nonprofit organization *More in Common* found that 86 percent of Americans were exhausted by how divided we have become as a country.[18] That means that almost all of us on both sides are frustrated with the nation's intensely polarized political discourse. And yet we haven't been able to figure out what to do about it.

During the writing of this book I encountered people who told me stories of how they have changed their leisure activities, their social circles—even their careers—because they could not stand the idea of coming into contact with people from the other political camp. It's no wonder that so many articles and podcasts have come out in the last few years about how important it is that we try to cure our nation's rift. The healing of America is far beyond the scope of this book, which is about surviving our social lives. However, I believe it is essential to our society as a whole that we keep talking to and socializing with the people who disagree with us.

No good can come of not talking to each other. Separation is not the answer. Otherizing is what causes more division, and ultimately, feeds hate. I have used terms like "the other side" throughout this book because that is indeed the pervasive feeling these days, but I am hoping that someday that phrase will go back to being used more frequently to describe a tennis court, or a person's face, or the moon. Maybe if we called each other donkeys and elephants, the silliness of those labels would cause a lightening up in our political discourse.

There are certainly enough real enemies for us to battle: ignorance, poverty, disease, corruption, pollution, and the biggest of all, fear. Seeing each other as the enemy—and getting into a shouting match at a retirement dinner, a holiday party, or a fundraiser—is never the answer. When you can have a conversation with someone you really disagree with, and at the end of it you both shake hands with respect and kindness, it is a kind of small miracle that almost feels like it could, in fact, begin to change the world.

We all have much more in common than we realize, and I have great faith in the future of our social well-being. There are new social organizations and clubs cropping up all over the place like "Make America Dinner Again" and "The People's Supper," whose purpose is to create spaces where people can air different views within an enjoyable, intelligent, and respectful atmosphere.

Welcoming conversations with people whose opinions differ from ours is actually the only way to begin to overcome the fear of the "other side." As Arthur C. Brooks says in his book *Love Your Enemies*, "The single biggest way a subversive can change America is not by disagreeing less, but by disagreeing better—engaging in earnest debate while still treating everyone with love and respect."

Unless those beneficent alien beings do come down to save us, which—as much as I have always been enamored of the idea—is fairly unlikely, we have no choice. We have to work on dispelling the conviction that people on the left and the right are enemies. At the very least we have to reject the idea that we can't enjoy each other's company.

So go forth, all ye hearty minglers. Remember: when mingling with the "enemy," there is nothing to fear, and everything to hope.

Acknowledgments

So many friends and acquaintances shared their ideas and their stories with me during the writing of this book that I cannot list them here; however, I am particularly indebted to first readers Amy Mintzer, Jason Harootunian, and Caroline Press whose feedback, contributions, and unflagging support were invaluable.

I'd also like to thank Reverend Schuyler Vogel, Senior Minister of the Fourth Universalist Society, and Dr. Jay Van Bavel, Associate Professor of Psychology at NYU, for allowing me to interview them for this book and for being so generous with their time.

I'm enormously grateful to all the hard-working folks at New Harbinger Publications, especially my editorial team, Jennye Garibaldi, Jennifer Holder, and Rona Bernstein.

Most of all, thanks to my wonderful agents, Gillian MacKenzie and Allison Devereux, for their belief in and excellent shepherding of this project.

Endnotes

1   "Partisanship and Political Animosity in 2016," Pew Research Center (June 22, 2016), 1.

2   Harlan Lebo, Surveying the Digital Future: *The 15th Annual Study on the Impact of Digital Technology on Americans* (Center for the Digital Future at USC Annenberg, 2017), 5.

3   Holly B. Shakya and Nicholas A. Christakis, "A New, More Rigorous Study Confirms: The More You Use Facebook, the Worse You Feel," *Harvard Business Review* (April 10, 2017), 2–5.

4   Hunt Allcott, Luca Braghieri, Sarah Eichmeyer, and Matthew Gentzkow, "The Welfare Effects of Social Media" (NBER Working Papers 25514, National Bureau of Economic Research, Inc., 2019), 5–15.

5   Matthias R. Mehl, Simine Vazire, Shannon E. Holleran, and C. Shelby Clark, "Eavesdropping on Happiness: Well-being is Related to Having Less Small Talk and More Substantive Conversations," *Psychological Science* 21, no. 4 (April 1, 2010), 539–41.

6   National Institute for Physiological Sciences, "Scientific Explanation to Why People Perform Better After Receiving a Compliment," *Science Daily* (November 9, 2012), 1–2.

7   "Sharply Divided U.S. Political Climate is Reflected in the Workplace," RandstandUSA.com (October 24, 2018).

8   "Leaders Who Can Laugh at Themselves Get a Thumbs Up," Association for Psychological Science (December 9, 2014), 1.

9   Hoang Nguyen, "Most Flat Earthers Consider Themselves Very Religious," YouGov.com (April 02, 2018).

10   Kit Smith, "53 Incredible Facebook Statistics and Facts," Brandwatch.com (June 1, 2019).

11   Kit Smith, "58 Incredible and Interesting Twitter Stats and Statistics," Brandwatch.com (January 3, 2019).

12   Mary Lister, "33 Mind-Boggling Instagram Stats & Facts for 2018," Wordstream.com (August 26, 2019).

13   Juliana Schroeder, Michael Kardas, and Nicholas Epley, "The Humanizing Voice: Speech Reveals, and Text Conceals, a More Thoughtful Mind in the Midst of Disagreement," *Psychological Science*, 28, no. 12 (2017), 1745–62.

14   Soroush Vosoughi, Deb Roy, and Sinan Aral, "The Spread of True and False News Online," *Science*, 359, no. 6380 (March 9, 2018), 1146–51.

15   Jason Szep, "'Go to Hell!' A Divided America Struggles to Heal After Ugly Election," Reuters.com (November 9, 2016).

16   Jennifer De Pinto, Fred Backus, and Anthony Salvanto, "Poll finds many Americans hope to avoid political discussions at Thanksgiving," CBSnews.com (November 21, 2018).

17   M. Keith Chen and Ryne Rohla, "The Effect of Partisanship and Political Advertising on Close Family Ties," *Science*, 360, no. 6392 (June 2018), 1020–24.

18   Stephen Hawkins, Daniel Yudkin, Miriam Juan-Torres, and Tim Dixon, "Hidden Tribes: Midterms Report," More in Common (November, 2018), 1.

Jeanne Martinet is author of eight other books, including *The Art of Mingling*, which has been published worldwide and has sold more than 150,000 copies in the US. She has been featured in *The New York Times*, *Salon*, *The Boston Globe*, the *Chicago Tribune*, and *The Washington Post*, as well as in many other publications. Martinet has shared her humor and mingling know-how on hundreds of TV and radio shows, including NBC's *The Today Show*, and NPR's *Morning Edition*. She lives, writes, and mingles in New York City, NY.

Real change *is* possible

For more than forty-five years, New Harbinger has published proven-effective self-help books and pioneering workbooks to help readers of all ages and backgrounds improve mental health and well-being, and achieve lasting personal growth. In addition, our spirituality books offer profound guidance for deepening awareness and cultivating healing, self-discovery, and fulfillment.

Founded by psychologist Matthew McKay and Patrick Fanning, New Harbinger is proud to be an independent, employee-owned company. Our books reflect our core values of integrity, innovation, commitment, sustainability, compassion, and trust. Written by leaders in the field and recommended by therapists worldwide, New Harbinger books are practical, accessible, and provide real tools for real change.

newharbingerpublications

MORE BOOKS *from*
NEW HARBINGER PUBLICATIONS

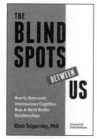

IT'S TIME TO TALK (& LISTEN)
How to Have Constructive Conversations About Race, Class, Sexuality, Ability & Gender in a Polarized World
9781684032679 / US $16.95

THE BLINDSPOTS BETWEEN US
How to Overcome Unconscious Cognitive Bias & Build Better Relationships
9781684035083 / US $16.95

MESSAGES, FOURTH EDITION
The Communication Skills Book
9781684031719 / US $21.95

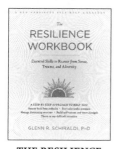

THE ASSERTIVENESS GUIDE FOR WOMEN
How to Communicate Your Needs, Set Healthy Boundaries & Transform Your Relationships
9781626253377 / US $16.95

ANXIETY HAPPENS
52 Ways to Find Peace of Mind
9781684031108 / US $14.95

THE RESILIENCE WORKBOOK
Essential Skills to Recover from Stress, Trauma & Adversity
9781626259409 / US $24.95

newharbingerpublications
1-800-748-6273 / newharbinger.com
(VISA, MC, AMEX / prices subject to change without notice)

Follow Us 📷 📘 📹 ▶ 📌 in

Don't miss out on new books in the subjects that interest you.
Sign up for our Book Alerts at **newharbinger.com/bookalerts**

DISCARD